"Nicholas Hamilton delivers an incredibly charming book full of high-proof wit while also providing a thoughtful, well-organized, and very creative manual of delicious cocktails. His love of the craft can be seen down to every detail, including the excellent pantry and tools introductory sections that every aspiring home bartender will appreciate."

—JON KUNG, author of *Kung Food*

Sipsy-Doozy

Sipsy-Doozy

100+ Respectfully Crafted Cocktails for the Home Bartender

Nicholas Hamilton

Art by Mike Falzone and Taylor Bourque

Countryman Press

An Imprint of W. W. Norton & Company
Independent Publishers Since 1923

* For my family, both given and chosen, who have
always believed in me. I hope I never do anything
to make you stop doing that. It feels nice.

For information about permission to reproduce selections
from this book, write to Permissions, Countryman Press,
500 Fifth Avenue, New York, NY 10110

For information about special discounts for bulk purchases,
please contact W. W. Norton Special Sales at
specialsales@wwnorton.com or 800-233-4830

Manufacturing by RRD Asia
Book design by Raphael Geroni
Art director: Allison Chi
Production manager: Devon Zahn

Countryman Press
www.countrymanpress.com

An imprint of W. W. Norton & Company, Inc.
500 Fifth Avenue, New York, NY 10110
www.wwnorton.com

ISBN: 978-1-68268-969-1

1 2 3 4 5 6 7 8 9 0

CONTENTS

True Classics—My Way 39

Mine—Hey, I Invented These! 63

FLAVOR TAGS ●

THE drinks in this book are "sorted" by their predominant flavors. The map that follows will encourage you to make a drink based on the tastes and sensations your tongue wants to taste and sense at that specific point in time. The "tag" (as we're calling them) listed first on any given recipe page is the primary flavor, what the consumer will primarily taste when drinking that cocktail. If you then follow the road map to find a cocktail that fits your drinker's desires, you should be splendid.

Alternatively, the tags are color coded and noted beside the recipes themselves. Feel free to rifle through the book, or better yet, use the index to find the ingredient you want to include, then use the tags to further educate yourself on the drink's taste profile before you make it.

● FRUITY

● BITTER

● SMOKY

● HERBAL

● FUNKY

● FLORAL

● COFFEE

● CREAMY

● HOT

As an actor, musician, and recently turned influencer *throwing up sounds*, you might expect Nicholas "Nic" Hamilton to be self-centered, spoiled, pretentious, annoying, egregious, dramatic, loud, maddening, and just downright disrespectful, but he swears you're only half right.

He makes drinks too.

So there's that.

INTRODUCTION

THE blurb on the adjacent page is a joke, of course. I pride myself on being respectful. In fact, a crowd-favorite running joke in my social media cocktail-making video series, the quote that gets repeated most often by viewers and commenters, is: "We'll clean up a little bit because we're respectful in this house."

You tell me, with a straight face, that those sound like words that would exit the mouth of a self-centered, spoiled, pretentious, annoying, egregious, dramatic, loud, maddening, and just downright disrespectful human being. Do it, I dare you.

But enough about me! Here's more about me:

When I was a kid, I *loved* to cook. Even as I entered the entertainment industry at age 11, it took a few more years for my fantasy of being a contestant on *Junior MasterChef Australia* to be eclipsed by much more achievable goals: Academy Award nominations, a star on the Hollywood Walk of Fame, etc. And while I do still enjoy blending flavors to create a dish that works in perfect balance and serving said dish in an aesthetically pleasing manner, when I turned 18, the legal drinking age in my home country of Australia, a new passion took over. I was drawn to an art form that, while it shared the flavor-melding characteristics and the earth-shattering-end-product-satisfaction of cooking, required less time, effort, and, most importantly, cleanup: drink-making.

Or mixology, if you'd like to be pretentious. Sometimes pretentiousness is okay! Pretentiousness in moderation, if you will. Still, I prefer the term *drink-making*.

When I finally graduated from high school and moved across the planet to Los Angeles, California (a feat I'd been yearning for since I'd started acting seven years prior), I rented a two-bedroom apartment in Mid-Wilshire, just below The Grove shopping complex. I finally felt independent, living in a space that was all my own. The first piece of furniture I bought for that apartment was my very own bar.

It was actually a 5½-foot-wide sideboard. Perhaps designed to hold picture frames and other family memorabilia, I saw it for no other purpose than storing glassware, bar tools, and bottles upon bottles of liquor. Throughout the following years, with the help of books by cocktail icons like David Wondrich, Dale DeGroff, and Sasha Petraske, and countless hours spent watching YouTube creators like Anders Erickson, Greg Titian (of *How to Drink*), Steven "Steve the Bartender" Roennfeldt, and Cara Devine (of *Behind the Bar* and manager of Bomba Rooftop in Melbourne, Australia) mix up hundreds of delicious-seeming elixirs, my drink-making skills became more enhanced. Until one day I decided to post a TikTok of me, dressed to the nines, making a Margarita Negra on that very same sideboard I'd purchased three years earlier.

And the rest, as they say, is history. (I've never loved that phrase. Was the rest of the story not also history? Confusing phrase.)

Ideally, the ensuing pages will make you fall as in love with cocktails as I have over the years. At the very least, I hope they make you go, "Oh, that's nice!" I'll settle for either.

HOW TO USE THIS BOOK ▲

IKE most hobbies, drink-making can prove expensive. My crochet-obsessed ex used to essentially hand his whole wallet to the cashier at Michael's. He once made a big plush corn cob, though. My point is, the money spent is often worth it.

One may see a recipe online or in a book that looks and sounds tasty, that handily uses an ingredient they already own, but then feel forced to immediately go out and buy the two to five other ingredients they lack (not including the novelty garnish) to enjoy a drink that evening. I feel this can scare off a lot of amateur mixologists from pursuing the craft any further.

I want nothing more than to ease you, dear reader, into the world in which I operate. The vast majority of the cocktails in this book are on the simpler side—tasty beverages that either require few ingredients or use components that are easy to make at home, such as the syrups found on page 23. You won't find any clarified cocktails in this book, nor any "foams" or overly scientific garnishes. I'll leave those for the next book.

Every recipe yields one drink. The bulk of the ingredients found in these recipes are fundamentals I believe every drink-maker should consistently have on their bar, with a few outliers thrown in here and there. The utmost "necessary" bottles and ingredients can be found in the **What to Use** section. More on that below.

I hope this book helps extinguish the myth that mixology must be expensive and complicated. It can be (especially further along your drink-making journey), but it doesn't have to be, at least not right away.

Another hopefully helpful facet of this book are the "tags" listed on each recipe. Feeling an herbal, floral, tart beverage? Perhaps a bitter, coffee, fruity cocktail? Rifle through the color-coded descriptors until you land on a drink that sounds like it should tickle your pickle. There's a **Flavor Tag Map** on pages 10–13 that should help you even further.

To that point, in this book there are a few more distinct sections:

The aforementioned encyclopedic **Stock Your Bar** section on page 19 details my substitutions and recommendations for the most common cocktail ingredients in this book. If there are no ingredient clarifications in the *Notes* portion of a recipe, check this section to ensure your cocktail tastes as close to intended as possible. Once you've made a cocktail using these recommendations, you can then tailor the drink to your own personal tongue.

The **True Classics** section holds 20 proper classic cocktails, alongside some fancy little QR codes that will link you to a short video of yours truly guiding you through how and why I make the tried-and-true classics we all adore. Find them on page 39.

There are four other sections at the beginning of this book dedicated to the making of any **Syrups** (page 23) or **Garnishes** (page 27), the performing of any **Techniques** (page 30), and the use of any **Glassware** (page 32) that appear in these pages. As mentioned, these are the simplest of syrups, garnishes, techniques, and glasses that the amateur drink-maker may need. Master the three former categories and use the recommended glasses and you'll be more like me. You know you want it.

I pray to Philip that you're able to make at least some of the drinks on the pages that follow. They're all worthy of your mouth and your throat.

On to the drinking . . .

STOCK YOUR BAR ■

O N E of the most common questions I get in the comment sections of my videos is, "I don't like/am allergic to/don't want to go out and buy ____ . What can I use instead?" While my first instinct is to always respond with, "Make a different drink!" I've been trying my hardest to be more forgiving lately, so here's a full encyclopedia of the most common recipe components in this book and substitutions for them, along with my favorite brands and styles of certain ingredients.

Follow these and the additional niche advice listed in the *Notes* section of each of the recipes, and your drink is more likely to taste just like mine. Alternatively, MAKE A DIFFERENT DRINK! (I did say I was *trying*.)

APPLE BRANDY

Recommendations: Laird's Applejack is the stock standard, and it's a fine option. If you happen to live in or near an orchard, perhaps do some exploring for another one.
Substitutions: Regular brandy/Cognac or an apple eau-de-vie.

AVERNA AMARO

Recommendations: Averna is a name-brand floral, herbal, bitter, orange-forward Italian amaro. It's an insanely delicious bottle that I would recommend any drinker have on their bar.
Substitutions: Cynar or Amaro Nonino.

BENEDICTINE

Recommendations: Benedictine is a name-brand herbal liqueur made from a closely guarded recipe of 27 different plants, herbs, and spices.
Substitutions: Yellow Chartreuse or Drambuie, if you *must*.

BITTERS

Recommendations: Bitters are extremely concentrated tinctures. Their usual job is to season a drink, to bring together the flavors and blend them, and there are many types. Aside from Angostura (the stock-standard aromatic bitters), the taste and quality of most of the bitters you'll find in this book won't hugely vary from brand to brand.
Substitutions: No substitutions. When found in dash form, bitters can be fully eliminated, but it's not recommended.

BRANDY (and Cognac and Armagnac)

Recommendations: Brandy is a distilled spirit most commonly made from grape juice, resulting in a raisin-like taste. I like St-Rémy and Lecarré. There are fancier brandies, like Cognac and Armagnac, named after the French regions in which they are made, that may elevate a brandy cocktail slightly, but they're mostly not necessary.
Substitutions: Again, Cognac or Armagnac are fancier options.

CAMPARI

Recommendations: Campari is a name-brand, bright red, bitter Italian liqueur.
Substitutions: A few brands have tried to emulate Campari's iconic flavor, but not many have succeeded. Just buy the real thing.

COFFEE

Recommendations: It's rare that I'll ever recommend using fresh espresso instead of cold brew or regular coffee that's been chilled, even in an **Espresso Martini** (page 44). If you want to do that, you absolutely can. Unless specifically recommended in a recipe (**Mezcal Dalnegroni;** page 143), stay away from instant coffee.

Substitutions: No substitutions; make something else.

COFFEE LIQUEUR

Recommendations: Mr Black or Tempus Fugit's Crème de Moka are my favorites. Stay away from Kahlúa and Tia Maria (essentially coffee syrups).

Substitutions: None.

CREAM OF COCONUT

Recommendations: Not to be confused with coconut milk, cream of coconut is a staple in tropical cocktails. You can make your own, but I've never seen the value in that, as store-bought is more than passable. Coco Lopez or Coco Reàl are both reputable brands.

Substitutions: High-quality coconut syrup. Coconut milk may be used but will need to be sweetened heavily to match the viscosity and richness of cream of coconut.

CRÈME LIQUEURS

Recommendations: Don't be fooled by the name, as crème in the cocktail world points to an ingredient's high sugar content and viscous texture rather than the inclusion of cream in said ingredient. Crème de banane, de cacao, de menthe, de mûre, and de violette all appear in this book. There are loads of brands. I usually stick with Tempus Fugit or Giffard, but feel free to shop around.

Substitutions: No real substitutions. Flavored syrups may be used in a pinch.

EGG WHITE

Recommendations: Egg white cocktails tend to scare people, but I encourage you to give them a try. I love the frothy texture you get with them. One tip: When separating the yolk from the white, do so over an empty shaker tin. That way, if you mess up, your cocktail isn't ruined.

Substitutions: If you're still not convinced, use a cocktail foamer (my fave is Fee Brothers' Fee Foam). You may have heard of people using aquafaba (the liquid in a can of chickpeas). I don't love doing this, it has an off-putting taste.

ELDERFLOWER LIQUEUR

Recommendations: Elderflower liqueur is humorously referred to as "bartender's ketchup" as a result of its versatility and approachability. The stock-standard elderflower liqueur has been St-Germain for as long as I can remember. The first bottle I bought, however, was from Fiorente and was equally delicious.

Substitutions: Nonalcoholic elderflower cordial/syrup. A similarly floral liqueur like crème de violette may work but will result in a different cocktail.

GIN

Recommendations: Gin is a distilled spirit flavored primarily with juniper berries and other botanicals, giving it a floral, herbal taste. I almost always use Tanqueray London Dry Gin, but there are so many others. Shop around. Some recipes in this book call for flavored and colored variations, like pink gin, butterfly pea flower, and sloe gin. Brand recommendations for those are in their *Notes* sections.

Substitutions: Flavored vodka. But don't.

LEMONS AND LIMES

Recommendations: As goes for most if not all fruit juice in cocktails, use only fresh lemon and lime juice. The bottled stuff contains additives beyond comprehension that make it taste like battery acid.

Substitutions: I personally think you can (mostly) use lemon and lime juice interchangeably, but still . . . it must be fresh.

MAPLE SYRUP

Recommendations: Contrary to popular belief, you shouldn't waste the best Grade A maple syrup in cocktails. The cheaper stuff is often more flavorful and breaks through in beverages much easier.

Substitutions: Honey syrup or regular sugar syrup, resulting in a different cocktail.

MARASCHINO LIQUEUR

Recommendations: Maraschino cherries are a classic cocktail garnish, but maraschino liqueur, made by distilling marasca cherries, can be easily overlooked. The cherry flavor and rich, syrupy texture can bring a wide variety of drinks up a whole 'nother level. Luxardo is the stock-standard brand.

Substitutions: Orange liqueur or another similarly fruity liqueur may be used, technically resulting in a different cocktail.

MEZCAL

Recommendations: It's commonly misconstrued that mezcal is a variant of tequila. In truth, all tequilas technically lie in the mezcal category. Mezcal is any distilled spirit made from any variety of agave, while tequila must be made from only the blue agave plant. Common mezcals can usually be distinguished by their intensely smoky flavor, caused by cooking the agave in pits in the ground. I'm not very well-versed in the world of different mezcals, but I like El Silencio Espadín and Ilegal Joven for cocktails.

Substitutions: Tequila can be subbed in for anyone who doesn't like the smoky flavor. Islay Scotch whisky is another smoky spirit that may work in a pinch.

ORANGE JUICE

Recommendations: A fairly rare ingredient in the world of mixology, as it can be overpowering, orange juice has to be perfectly balanced to make a coherent cocktail. As I do with most fruit juices, I recommend freshly squeezing your own orange juice and straining out the pulp before you measure it. If you can find a reputable pulpless orange juice in a bottle, you may use it at your own risk. Also, fun fact: I think I'm allergic to orange juice? The jury's out, but it does make my tongue feel fuzzy.

Substitutions: No real substitutions. Pineapple or grapefruit juice may work but will likely make the drink too tart or too bitter.

ORANGE LIQUEUR

Recommendations: Most orange liqueurs are fairly similar; I'd just urge you to buy a high-quality bottle. Cointreau, Pierre Ferrand's Dry Curaçao, Luxardo's Triplum Triple Sec, and Grand Marnier are all great options.

Substitutions: Another fruity liqueur could be used as a substitute, but I strongly recommend getting a bottle of orange liqueur. It's a bar staple.

PINEAPPLE JUICE

Recommendations: Pineapple juice is one of the only fruit juices I don't recommend freshly squeezing. The stuff in the cans is as good as long as it's 100 percent pineapple juice, not from concentrate.

Substitutions: None. It seems a lot of people are allergic to pineapple juice. If that's you, make something else.

RUM

Recommendations: Rum is a spirit distilled from fermented sugarcane juice or molasses. It's well known to be my favorite spirit category. The funkier the better, in my opinion, but multiple drinks in this book call for a specific type. For a *tame dark rum* (used in most rum recipes), shoot for Hamilton Demerara or a Puerto Rican rum, like Ron del Barrilito. For *white rum* (used to maintain the color of a drink), use a rum that's been aged and then charcoal filtered to keep the flavor, like The Real McCoy 3 Year or a similar, fruity spirit like Clear Water's Lorenz. In the *funky rum* category, I loooove Hamilton Jamaican Pot Still Black. Angostura 1919 and Smith & Cross are also great options.
Substitutions: No substitutions.

SODA WATER

Recommendations: Carbonated water can be made at home or bought in bottles. I like Topo Chico, but most are the same. Club soda, seltzer, and soda water are all mostly interchangeable.
Substitutions: Flavored soda water can work in some instances; a hard seltzer if you're feeling naughty. Tonic water does taste different, but give it a try if that's what you have on hand.

TEQUILA

Recommendations: Tequila is a distilled spirit made from the blue agave plant. Blanco tequila is unaged and can get overpowered easily. I don't love using Añejo (extra aged) tequila in cocktails, as it can trample the other ingredients. I'll almost always reach for a reposado, a middle ground, for the perfect blend of flavors.

Espolòn and Don Julio are good options, just steer clear of celebrity brands.
Substitutions: No substitutions.

VERMOUTH

Recommendations: Vermouth is fortified wine, so, like wine, there is a wide array of vermouths. Dry, sweet, and blanc vermouth all appear in this book, all to achieve different tastes. I like Carpano Antica for sweet vermouth and Dolin for dry and blanc, but there are a bunch of options. Steer clear of Martini brand.
Substitutions: Sherry and port can be used as substitutions, but it's not recommended. Vermouth is usually very cheap. Get a small bottle and store it in the fridge.

VODKA

Recommendations: Vodka is a clear, neutral distilled spirit. Vodka is vodka. Get literally any unflavored brand on the market. Literally. Any. Brand.
Substitutions: Substituting out vodka for another clear liquor in vodka cocktails can be fun. Try it out so you don't have to use vodka.

WHISKEY

Recommendations: Whiskey is a spirit distilled from fermented grains. There are many, many types. Don't go for an expensive bottle when mixing with whiskey—it's a waste. It's also rare a type of whiskey matters in any specific cocktail, but here are my mixing faves in every category. *Bourbon:* Buffalo Trace and Four Roses. *Rye:* Templeton and Rittenhouse. *Blended Scotch:* Dewar's White Label and Monkey Shoulder. *Irish:* Jameson and Tullamore D.E.W. *Japanese:* Suntory Toki and Akashi White Oak. *Islay Scotch:* Caol Ila 12 Year and Laphroaig 10 Year.
Substitutions: No substitutions.

SYRUPS ▲

HOMEMADE syrups are not only cheaper to make than buying plastic squeeze bottles of them at grocery or liquor stores, but they're always *much* more trustworthy in terms of their ingredients and methods of creation. You know exactly what you have put in your pots and pans to make your syrups, and once you have a syrup recipe you know and love, you can create it exactly like that, time and time again, to create consistently banging cocktails.

If you're feeling lazy, store-bought syrups *can* be okay. Just look out for any artificial flavors or high-fructose corn syrup. I recommend Liber & Co.

If you're worried you won't use all your syrup before its expiration date, add ½ ounce vodka once cooled. This adds two months of shelf life.

SIMPLE SYRUP

1 part white sugar

1 part water

Add white sugar and water to saucepan.

Heat until sugar dissolves.

Turn off heat and allow to cool.

Bottle and refrigerate. Use within a month.

DEMERARA SYRUP

1 part demerara/ raw sugar

1 part water

Add demerara sugar and water to saucepan.

Heat until sugar dissolves.

Turn off heat and allow to cool.

Bottle and refrigerate. Use within a month.

GRENADINE

1½ cups sugar

1 cup pomegranate juice

½ teaspoon pomegranate molasses

¼ teaspoon rose water

Add sugar, pomegranate juice, and pomegranate molasses to saucepan.

Heat until sugar dissolves.

Turn off heat and allow to cool.

Add rose water and stir to combine.

Bottle and refrigerate. Use within a month.

* Grenadine can be subbed out for any berry syrup in most scenarios.

ORGEAT

1½ cups sugar

1 cup unsweetened almond milk

2 teaspoons orange blossom water

1 teaspoon rose water

1 teaspoon almond extract

Add sugar and almond milk to saucepan.

Simmer until sugar dissolves, ensuring milk does not scald.

Turn off heat and allow to cool.

Add orange blossom water, rose water, and almond extract and stir to combine.

Bottle and refrigerate. Use within a month.

HONEY SYRUP

3 parts honey

1 part hot water

Add honey and water to container.

Shake until honey dissolves.

Refrigerate. Use within 3 months.

BERRY SYRUP

1 cup sugar

1 cup water

8 ounces (225 g) berries (sliced, if strawberries)

Add sugar, water, and berries to saucepan.

Heat until sugar dissolves.

Gently simmer for 30 minutes.

Turn off heat and allow to cool.

Bottle and refrigerate. Use within 2 to 3 weeks.

CINNAMON SYRUP

1 cup sugar

1 cup water

4 or 5 cinnamon sticks

Add sugar, water, and cinnamon to saucepan.

Heat until sugar dissolves.

Gently simmer for 30 minutes.

Turn off heat and allow to cool.

Bottle with the used cinnamon sticks and refrigerate. Use within 2 to 3 weeks.

ROSEMARY SYRUP

1 cup sugar

1 cup water

3 rosemary sprigs

Add sugar, water, and rosemary to saucepan.

Heat until sugar dissolves.

Gently simmer for 30 minutes.

Turn off heat and allow to cool.

Bottle and refrigerate. Use within 2 to 3 weeks.

GINGER SYRUP

1 cup sugar

1 cup water

8 ounces (225 g) ginger, peeled and sliced

Add sugar, water, and ginger to saucepan.

Heat until sugar dissolves.

Gently simmer for 30 minutes.

Turn off heat and allow to cool.

Strain and, if you wish, save ginger to use as a garnish (see page 27).

Bottle syrup and refrigerate. Use within 2 to 3 weeks.

JALAPEÑO SYRUP

1 cup sugar

1 cup water

8 ounces (225 g) jalapeños, sliced

Add sugar, water, and jalapeños to saucepan.

Heat until sugar dissolves.

Gently simmer for 30 minutes.

Turn off heat and allow to cool.

Strain and, if you wish, save jalapeños to use as a garnish (see page 27).

Bottle syrup and refrigerate. Use within 2 to 3 weeks.

GARNISHES ●

LET'S be honest. The only garnishes that truly matter are those that affect the drink's aroma or taste. Most garnishes lie in this category and are integral to the cocktail's final form, but some should be reserved purely to impress dinner guests or make your Instagram Story slightly prettier.

The garnishes in this section are distinguished using this factor: novelty or necessary.

CITRUS SWATH (Necessary)

Peel one vertical length of a citrus using a peeler. With the exterior of the peel facing the cocktail, squeeze the peel over the drink to express the citrus oils. Place in drink, on rim, or discard.

This garnish gives the cocktail a citrusy aroma that should complement the flavors of the cocktail.

CITRUS WHEEL (Novelty)

Cut citrus in half. Cut a wheel that is thick enough to stand on its own when placed on the glass's rim without flopping over. Cut a slit from the middle of the wheel to the edge. Place on rim of glass.

Instruct drinker *not* to squeeze wheel into cocktail.

CITRUS WEDGE (Necessary)

Cut citrus into eighths. Make a slit halfway across one wedge. Place on rim of glass.

Instruct drinker to squeeze wedge into drink before stirring and consuming.

CITRUS BOWL (Novelty and Necessary)

Completely invert used citrus half so the exterior forms a bowl shape. Ensure there are no holes in the citrus bowl.

This garnish is usually placed on top of a cocktail, then filled with alcohol and lit on fire before being extinguished and pushed into the drink. Used only in the Mai Tai (page 47).

ABSINTHE RINSE (Necessary)

Add ¼ ounce (7.5 ml) absinthe to glass. Roll glass around so absinthe coats the inside. Pour out excess. Alternatively, use an atomizer to avoid waste.

While not technically a garnish, the rinsing of absinthe allows for the taste and aroma of the intense spirit to come through without overpowering a balanced cocktail.

BITTERS SWIRL (Novelty and Necessary)

Add drops of aromatic or Peychaud's bitters on the surface of the drink. Swirl a cocktail pick through the bitters to achieve desired marbled effect.

Seen used as a garnish on some of the sours in this book, the bitters swirl is an aesthetically pleasing way to mask the harmless smell some egg white drinks may have.

CANDIED GINGER/JALAPEÑO (Necessary)

Make ginger or jalapeño syrup (see page 25). Place used ginger or jalapeño on a foil-covered baking tray. While still warm, cover in demerara/raw sugar, ensuring every slice is coated. Leave for at least 24 hours, until completely dry, before storing in airtight jar or container.

Place 2 to 3 slices on a cocktail pick and serve with drink.

COCKTAIL PICK (Necessary)

Add garnish on a cocktail pick. Lay cocktail pick across the rim of the glass.

Instruct drinker to snack on garnish before, during, or after consuming the cocktail.

COFFEE BEANS (Novelty)

Place three coffee beans in the center of the drink's surface in a tight circle.

This practice originated in Italy, with sambuca commonly being served with three coffee beans to represent health, wealth, and happiness. It's become a novel way of serving Espresso Martinis and their riffs.

CUCUMBER SLICE (Necessary)

Cut a slice of cucumber, about ¼ inch thick. Cut a slit in the slice to allow it to be placed on the glass's rim.

Instruct drinker to snack on the cucumber as they enjoy their cocktail.

FRESHLY GRATED (Necessary)

Using a zester, grate ingredient over the top of the drink.

This garnish allows one to smell the aroma of the freshly grated garnish as they drink. Freshly grated spices are always preferable to the pre-ground, bottled stuff.

MARASCHINO CHERRY (Necessary)

Add one or two maraschino cherries on a cocktail pick and rest it on top of the drink.

Don't buy the bright red maraschino cherries. You're looking for a deep purple color, like Luxardo's.

MINT (Necessary)

Wash and dry a plume of mint. Slap to express oils. Insert into drink.

Ensure a straw is placed close enough to the plume to influence the aroma as the drinker consumes the cocktail.

RIMMING (Necessary—don't be crass!)

Place ingredient (often sugar or salt) on plate. Moisten half of the outside rim of a glass with the interior of a citrus fruit. Roll glass in rimming ingredient, coating half the rim and some of the side of the glass.

Only rimming half a glass allows the drinker to take sips both with and without the taste of the rimming ingredient.

PINEAPPLE FRONDS (Novelty)

Remove the fronds from a head of pineapple and insert into drink. This can give off a cheeky little island vibe.

TECHNIQUES ◼

I T'S important for a drink-maker to be as comfortable as humanly possible as they concoct beverages. If they're not, the drinker can taste it in the cocktail. It's like a horse smelling fear. That being said, I'm not here to tell you exactly which techniques to use when making drinks. If you have drink-concocting methods that work for you, be my guest. If you're just starting out and/or haven't perfected your techniques, allow this to be your very rough guide.

DRY SHAKING (without ice)

If using a two-tin shaker (preferred): Construct beverage in small shaker tin. Pour liquid into big shaker tin and insert small tin into big tin. Smack bottom of small tin to form a watertight seal between the tins. Slowly shake for 5 seconds, ensuring a proper seal is formed. Grasp shaker with both hands, securing both tins, and vigorously shake for 15 seconds. Smack shaker where the tins meet to break the seal and open the shaker.

If using a cobbler shaker: Construct beverage in shaker. Place lid on top, ensuring a proper seal is formed, before adding shaker cap on top. Grasp shaker with both hands, securing lid and cap, and vigorously shake for 15 seconds. Hit cap sideways to break the seal and remove the shaker lid.

SHAKING (with ice)

If using a two-tin shaker (preferred): Construct beverage in small shaker tin. Add one scoop of regular ice and one large ice cube to big shaker tin. Pour liquid into big shaker tin and insert small tin into big tin. Smack bottom of small tin to form a watertight seal between the tins. Slowly shake for 5 seconds, ensuring a proper seal is formed. Grasp shaker with both hands, securing both tins, and vigorously shake for 15 seconds. Smack shaker where the tins meet to break the seal and open the shaker.

If using a cobbler shaker: Construct beverage in shaker. Carefully add one scoop of regular ice and one large ice cube to shaker. Place lid on top, ensuring a proper seal is formed, before adding shaker cap on top. Grasp shaker with a firm hold on lid and cap and vigorously shake for 15 seconds. Hit cap sideways to break the seal and remove the shaker lid.

DOUBLE STRAINING

If using a two-tin shaker (preferred): After shaking the cocktail, ensure liquid is in the big shaker tin. Place strainer on top of big shaker tin. Strain drink through both it and a fine drink strainer/sieve into the glass.

If using a cobbler shaker: Strain cocktail into the glass through both the supplied strainer in the shaker's lid and a fine drink strainer.

STIRRING

Construct cocktail in mixing glass. Add ice to completely fill mixing glass. Insert long barspoon and stir for 15 to 20 seconds or until chilled and diluted. Insert julep strainer (or Hawthorne strainer, both work) and strain into glass.

MUDDLING

Using a muddler, press down on ingredients in shaker or glass (highball or rocks, not a stemmed glass, for safety). If muddling mint, ensure not to over-muddle or twist the muddler, as this will rip and bruise the mint. When muddling most other ingredients, twisting the muddler is usually acceptable.

RINSING

To rinse a glass is to coat the inside of the glass before the cocktail is poured in, to influence the aroma of the drink. To do so, add ¼ ounce (7.5 ml) liquid to the glass and turn it so the liquid fully coats the interior of the glass. Pour out the excess.

Optionally, you may use an atomizer to spray the interior of a glass, achieving full coverage without waste.

FLOATING

To float a liquid on top of a cocktail, ensure the floating liquid is less dense than the drink. Lay a barspoon face up just above the surface of the drink. Gently pour liquid over the barspoon onto the drink.

DUMPING

Instead of straining, just pour the drink (shaken ice and all) straight into the glass. Commonly used in Piña Colada riffs and cocktails where the flavor of the ice is intentional (**Dad's Tea**, page 173).

GLASSWARE ▲

WHILE it's mostly true that a cocktail can be served in a bucket and still taste pretty much the same, there are a few positives to serving a drink in the "right" glassware. Each recipe in this book has a glassware preference in the *Method*, so here are the reasons why you should use each specific glass type and my recommendations for each. Again, if you only have your favorite mug on hand, the world won't end.

LOWBALL

Also known as a tumbler, rocks, or Old Fashioned glass, the lowball glass is sturdy yet classy. It's used mostly for short boozy drinks that need dilution, like the **Old Fashioned** (page 54), the **Negroni** (page 53), and their riffs, but I also like serving my sours in a lowball. If I don't want to get too buzzed, I'll often serve a "coupe cocktail" in one over ice, to increase dilution.

The lowball is a home bar necessity and most are one and the same, but some are more pleasant to drink out of than others. It's less about aesthetic here and more about performance. My favorites are short and stout tumblers, which increase the amount of contact the drink has with the surface area of the ice and help the aromas reach my nose easier.

You may see reference of a "double rocks glass." This is just a bigger lowball, recommended so the drink fits. Feel free to just use a double rocks glass for all rocks cocktails, or scale the larger drink down.

HIGHBALL/COLLINS

Most bubbly cocktails are served in tall, skinny glasses called highballs or Collins glasses. These glasses are larger in volume than most and allow for a drink to be lengthened with nonalcoholic mixers, like in the **Action Royale** (page 76) and the **Dirty Shirley** (page 74).

Along with the rocks glass, this is the other glassware staple you should stock in your home bar. Beware of getting too big of a highball.

Anything larger than 12 ounces (360 ml), when "topped" with mixer, will result in a weak cocktail.

COUPE

The coupe not only looks fancy and adds a touch of sophistication to a cocktail, it also enhances aromas and allows a sweaty-palmed drinker to maintain a drink's cold temperature by holding the glass by the stem. To that point, it's very important to serve the drink in a coupe that has been chilled prior, as there isn't any ice to keep the drink cold. Put the glass in the freezer for at least 5 minutes before serving.

My favorite coupe is the Nick and Nora glass. It's small and dainty and very satisfying to drink out of. Most, if not all, drinks in this book that list a coupe as the preferred vessel were originally served in a Nick and Nora.

TODDY/MUG

Referenced in this book when serving almost any hot cocktail, the toddy glass is a tempered, mug-like, handled glass that allows the drinker to consume the beverage without burning their hand.

While not transparent, ceramic mugs are absolutely fine options for all hot cocktails. A drink like the **Irish Coffee** (page 46) and its riffs may falter slightly, as the striking look of the hot coffee cocktail layer compared to the white cream layer is half the fun, but don't stress about it.

HURRICANE/WINE

Used in this book for the **Piña Colada** (page 57) and its many riffs, the hurricane glass is my go-to receptacle when serving any "dumped" drink (see page 31). You may use any wineglass for this exact purpose, or any large glass, for that matter.

GIBRALTAR/SNIFTER

The **Sazerac** (page 58) and its riffs use a chilled Gibraltar glass or snifter to preserve a stirred drink's temperature without having to use ice, much like a coupe glass. It's a fine, classic option and looks *gorgeous*, but a coupe or a chilled rocks glass works as an absolutely fine substitute.

CHAMPAGNE FLUTE

Used for sparkling wine cocktails like the **B2P2** (page 103), this tall, skinny wineglass is completely unnecessary, used mostly for aesthetics. Drinkers are more likely to own a wineglass and should use that instead if so.

KEY TO ILLUSTRATIONS ●

TECHNIQUE

Built Cocktail

Shaken Cocktail

Stirred Cocktail

ALCOHOL

Beer

Coffee Liqueur

Blanc Vermouth

Whiskey, Demerara Rum, Funky Rum

Champagne/ Sparkling Wine

Cider

Irish Cream Liqueur, Mezcal

Averna Amaro

Dry Vermouth

Green Chartreuse

Crème de Cacao, Overproof Rum, Vodka, White Rum

Amaretto Liqueur, Apple Brandy, Benedictine, Brandy, Mead, Metaxa, Southern Comfort

Absinthe, Crème de Menthe, Gin, Umeshu Plum Liqueur

Orange Liqueur

Grapefruit Liqueur, Pink Gin, Rose Gin

Port Wine, Sherry

Butterfly Pea Flower Gin, Crème de Mûre, Sloe Gin

Aperol, Campari, Maraschino Liqueur

Red Wine

Blue Curaçao

Sake

Sweet Vermouth

Tequila

Crème de Banane, Elderflower Liqueur, Lemon Vodka, Suze

BITTERS

Aromatic Bitters

CBD Bitters

Cocoa Bitters

Lavender Bitters

Orange Bitters

Peychaud's Bitters

SYRUPS & JUICES

Apple Juice

Blackberry Syrup

Blueberry Syrup

Chocolate Syrup

Cinnamon Syrup

Cranberry Juice

Demerara Syrup

Ginger Syrup

Grapefruit Juice

Grenadine

Hibiscus Syrup

Honey Syrup

Jalapeño Syrup

Lemon Juice

Lime Juice

Maple Syrup

Maraschino Cherry Syrup

Orange Juice

Orgeat Syrup

Pineapple Juice

Raspberry Syrup

Rosemary Syrup

Simple Syrup

Strawberry Syrup

Yuzu Juice

MIXERS, GARNISHES & MISCELLANEOUS

Aquafaba

Whole Egg

Hot Water

Peppermint Tea

Cinnamon

Egg Yolk

Lapsang Souchong Tea

Red Bull

Coffee

English Breakfast Tea

Lemon-Lime Soda

Rose Water

Cola

Ginger Ale

Lime Sections

Salt

Cream of Coconut

Ginger Beer

Maraschino Cherry

Soda Water

Cucumber

Hot Sauce

Milk, Half-and-Half, Heavy Cream

Sugar Cube

Earl Grey Tea

Vanilla Ice Cream

Mint Leaves

Vanilla Extract

Egg White

Jam/Jelly

Peanut Butter

True Classics

—My Way

Classic cocktails, to me, have always been the most fascinating topic in the subject of mixology. Drinks that, in some instances, have survived for over 200 years. They're so good that the recipes have been handed down from generation to generation and riffed on until there are seemingly no riffs left.

This section includes some of these classic cocktails as well as some more modern creations I've tried over the years and loved enough to include in this book.

You'll find that, while these recipes were first made by another (often ancient) drink-maker, a lot of the ratios vary from the original specs (recipes), the ones scribed by their creators. They've been workshopped by yours truly to create a drink that *my* mouth would like to touch multiple times.

You see, every drinker has their "perfect" list of ingredients, ratios, and procedures for so many of these recipes. The beautiful thing about mixology, aside from the drinking, is how one individual's "classic" cocktail recipe could taste so very different from another's. Drink-makers love to drink, and we love others who love to drink what *they* love to drink.

So please, don't take these recipes as the holy grail. Try them. If the drink sparks even an ounce (or milliliter) of enjoyment, then experiment. Experiment with the ratios. Experiment with the ingredients. Experiment with the processes. Experiment until you eventually find a drink that satisfies your tongue. Every. Tongue. Is. Different.

Anyway, enough tongue talk.

Let's just go ahead and do it.

Bramble

The Bramble is a gin fix that's served over crushed ice before being doused in rich crème de mûre, a jammy blackberry liqueur. It influenced **Classy Boy** (page 80) and **Top Hat and a Hat Tan** (page 93).

INGREDIENTS

2 ounces (60 ml) gin

1 ounce (30 ml) lemon juice, freshly squeezed

¼ ounce (7.5 ml) simple syrup (see page 23)

½ ounce (15 ml) crème de mûre (blackberry liqueur)

METHOD

Add the gin, lemon juice, and simple syrup to a shaker.

Half-fill a double rocks glass with crushed ice.

Add ice to shaker and shake until chilled.

Strain mixture into prepared glass and top with more crushed ice.

Pour crème de mûre into drink to create a marbled effect.

Cosmopolitan

Made even more famous by *Sex and the City*, the Cosmo was originally popularized by Dale DeGroff, head of the modern cocktail renaissance and my personal favorite mixologist. The light, fruity drink influenced **Gabe's Blueberry Cosmopolitan** (page 100).

INGREDIENTS

1 ounce (30 ml) vodka

1 ounce (30 ml) orange liqueur

1¼ ounces (37.5 ml) cranberry juice

¼ ounce (7.5 ml) lime juice, freshly squeezed

Lime wheel, to garnish (see page 27)

METHOD

Add the vodka, orange liqueur, cranberry juice, and lime juice to a shaker.

Add ice and shake until chilled.

Double strain into a chilled coupe glass.

Garnish with a lime wheel.

Daiquiri

A proper Daiquiri, contrary to popular belief, is a bare-bones Rum Fix. If you order a traditional Daiquiri and it comes out frozen, leave that bar immediately and go somewhere that respects you. Traditionally made with a regular simple or demerara syrup, any syrup of your choosing may be used here, turning it into a flavored Daiquiri.

INGREDIENTS

2 ounces (60 ml) rum

1 ounce (30 ml) demerara syrup (see page 23)

1 ounce (30 ml) lime juice, freshly squeezed

Lime wheel, to garnish (see page 27)

METHOD

Add the rum, demerara syrup, and lime juice to a shaker.

Add ice and shake until chilled.

Double strain into a chilled coupe glass.

Garnish with a lime wheel.

Eggnog

A flip cocktail uses a whole egg. The most well-known of them, Eggnog, is a holiday classic that tastes like drinkable custard, not to say that custard isn't already drinkable. My version of a flip, the **Flipsy-Doozy**, is on page 170.

INGREDIENTS

2 ounces (60 ml) bourbon

½ ounce (15 ml) maraschino liqueur

½ ounce (15 ml) simple syrup (see page 23)

1 egg

Freshly grated nutmeg, to garnish (see page 28)

METHOD

Add the bourbon, maraschino liqueur, simple syrup, and egg to a shaker.

Dry shake until emulsified, 15 seconds.

Add ice and shake until chilled.

Double strain into a chilled coupe glass.

Garnish with freshly grated nutmeg.

Espresso Martini

A modern classic, the Espresso Martini may be the most popular cocktail on the planet at the time of writing. Don't be fooled by the name, for the early 2000s birthed the idea that any drink served in a martini glass should be named as such. Silly. The Espresso Martini inspired the **Affogato Martini** (page 125), **Banane Noire** (page 134), and **Post-Nut Clarity** (page 137).

INGREDIENTS

1 ounce (30 ml) coffee liqueur

¾ ounce (22.5 ml) vodka

1¼ ounces (37.5 ml) coffee/espresso, chilled

½ ounce (30 ml) simple syrup (see page 23)

3 coffee beans, to garnish (see page 28)

METHOD

Add the coffee liqueur, vodka, coffee, and simple syrup to a shaker.

Dry shake until emulsified, 15 seconds.

Add ice and shake until chilled.

Double strain into a chilled coupe glass.

Garnish with 3 coffee beans.

Hot Toddy

My recipe for this warming cup of liquored-up lemon-honey tea is bolstered by smoky Islay Scotch whisky. I've riffed on it further to create **Dreary Day's Night** (page 194) and **Sloe Is Calm, Calm Is Sloe** (page 193).

INGREDIENTS

¾ ounce (22.5 ml) Islay Scotch whisky

¾ ounce (22.5 ml) blended Scotch whisky

1 English Breakfast tea bag

1 ounce (30 ml) honey syrup (see page 24)

½ ounce (30 ml) lemon juice, freshly squeezed

4 ounces (120 ml) boiling water

Lemon wheel, to garnish (see page 27)

Cinnamon stick, for stirring (optional)

METHOD

Add the Islay Scotch, blended Scotch, tea bag, honey syrup, and lemon juice to a toddy glass or mug.

Add boiling water and stir with optional cinnamon stick until combined.

Garnish with a lemon wheel, leaving tea bag and cinnamon stick in.

Irish Coffee

I had my first proper Irish Coffee at the Buena Vista Café in San Francisco, a bar that has since become synonymous with the hot layered cocktail, and I've yet to look back. The **London Fog** (page 106) was inspired by this classic.

INGREDIENTS

1 ounce (30 ml) Irish whiskey

3½ ounces (105 ml) brewed hot coffee

½ ounce (15 ml) simple syrup (see page 23)

½ ounce (15 ml) heavy cream

Freshly grated nutmeg, to garnish (see page 28)

METHOD

Add the Irish whiskey, coffee, and simple syrup to a small mug and stir until combined.

Float with heavy cream (see page 31).

Garnish with freshly grated nutmeg.

Mai Tai

A proper early 1900s classic tropical cocktail, the Mai Tai is not only banging but allows one to light their drink on fire. And that's always fun. For a beer-centric riff, try the **Tai One On** (page 90).

INGREDIENTS

1½ ounces (45 ml) rum

½ ounce (15 ml) orange liqueur

1 ounce (30 ml) orgeat (see page 24)

¾ ounce (22.5 ml) lime juice, freshly squeezed (reserve used lime halves)

½ ounce (15 ml) overproof rum

Pineapple fronds, to garnish (see page 28)

Lime wheel, to garnish (see page 27)

Maraschino cherry, to garnish (optional; see page 28)

METHOD

Fill a double rocks glass halfway with crushed ice.

Add the rum, orange liqueur, orgeat, and lime juice to shaker.

Add ice and shake until chilled.

Strain into prepared glass and top with more crushed ice.

Take one used lime half and turn it inside out, so the lime exterior forms a bowl shape.

Place the lime bowl in the center of the drink's surface. Add a maraschino cherry to the lime bowl, if desired, and fill the bowl with overproof rum.

Garnish the cocktail with pineapple fronds and a lime wheel.

Light overproof rum in lime bowl on fire. Extinguish flame by pushing lime bowl into drink before consuming.

Manhattan

The Manhattan is so simple, yet it manages to make me giddy every time I consume it. The Manhattan inspired the following drinks: the **No Takesies-Backsies** (page 160), **Tapsalteerie** (page 69), and **Wishful Drinking** (page 182).

INGREDIENTS

2 ounces (60 ml) whiskey

1 ounce (30 ml) sweet vermouth

2 dashes aromatic bitters

2 dashes orange bitters

Maraschino cherry, to garnish (see page 28)

METHOD

Add the whiskey, sweet vermouth, aromatic bitters, and orange bitters to a mixing glass.

Add ice and stir until chilled and diluted, 15 to 20 seconds.

Strain into a chilled coupe glass.

Garnish with a maraschino cherry.

Margarita

Neither a Mezcalita nor a proper Margarita, this recipe is *not* traditional, but it is my favorite version of the deliciously simple classic. This book holds two Margarita riffs: **Crepusculo** (page 135) and **Debbie Did It** (page 145).

INGREDIENTS

1½ ounces (45 ml) tequila

½ ounce (15 ml) mezcal

½ ounce (15 ml) orange liqueur

¾ ounce (22.5 ml) lime juice, freshly squeezed

¾ ounce (22.5 ml) demerara syrup (see page 23)

Lime wheel, to garnish (see page 27)

METHOD

Add the tequila, mezcal, orange liqueur, lime juice, and demerara syrup to a shaker.

Add ice and shake until chilled.

Double strain into an ice-filled rocks glass, half-rimmed with salt or Tajín (see page 28).

Garnish with a lime wheel.

Martini

This is true for all these classics, but I'll reiterate it here: This is *my* favorite version of the Martini. Many may call it a Wet Martini, which is true, as it holds more vermouth than is "typical." Both the **Attaché** (page 112) and the **Philip** (page 111) take inspiration from this one.

INGREDIENTS

2 ounces (60 ml) gin

¾ ounce (22.5 ml) blanc vermouth

3 dashes orange bitters

Lemon swath, to garnish (see page 27)

METHOD

Add all ingredients to a mixing glass.

Add ice and stir until chilled and diluted, 15 to 20 seconds.

Strain into a chilled coupe glass.

Garnish with an expressed lemon swath.

Mojito

Coined the Slow Mojito by Anders Erickson, my favorite version of the traditional Mojito takes a significant amount of time and effort, but it is well, *well* worth it. Follow these instructions/this video closely and thank me later.

INGREDIENTS

10 to 12 mint leaves

1 tablespoon demerara/ raw sugar

½ lime, quartered

2 ounces (60 ml) rum

3 ounces (90 ml) soda water

Mint sprig, to garnish (see page 28)

Lime wheel, to garnish (see page 27)

METHOD

Add the mint leaves and demerara sugar to a highball glass.

Stir for at least 1 minute, bringing the mint and sugar up the sides of the glass as you stir.

Add lime sections. Gently muddle, juicing the lime but not pulverizing the mint.

Add rum and fill glass with ice.

Top with soda water. Stir until incorporated.

Garnish with a mint sprig and a lime wheel.

Moscow Mule

The first cocktail I mastered (not a difficult task), the Moscow Mule is a simple highball, traditionally served in a completely unnecessary copper mug. For my riffs, see **Tub-Thumper** (page 165) and **Mule Ride in the Orchard** (see note on page 154).

INGREDIENTS

2 ounces (60 ml) vodka

2 dashes orange bitters

1 dash aromatic bitters

½ ounce (15 ml) lime juice, freshly squeezed

6 ounces (180 ml) ginger beer

Lime wedge, to garnish (see page 27)

METHOD

Add the vodka, orange bitters, aromatic bitters, and lime juice to an ice-filled copper mug and stir until combined.

Top with ginger beer.

Garnish with a lime wedge.

Negroni

People have tried to improve the already perfect, classically simple Negroni for years. Alas, the bittersweet, equal-parts sipper is faultless, no notes. **Honey, I Made a Drink** (page 186), **Hamilton Special** (page 156), and **Mezcal Dalnegroni** (page 143) all take inspiration.

INGREDIENTS

1 ounce (30 ml) gin

1 ounce (30 ml) sweet vermouth

1 ounce (30 ml) Campari

Orange swath, to garnish (see page 27)

METHOD

Add the gin, sweet vermouth, and Campari to a mixing glass.

Add ice and stir until chilled and diluted, 15 to 20 seconds.

Strain into an ice-filled rocks glass.

Garnish with an expressed orange swath.

Old Fashioned

Perhaps (almost definitely) the oldest drink in the book, the Old Fashioned is a good way to drink whatever whiskey you have that isn't good enough to be drunk neat.

INGREDIENTS

1 sugar cube

4 dashes aromatic bitters

2 dashes orange bitters

Maraschino cherry, to garnish (see page 28)

Orange swath, to garnish (see page 27)

METHOD

Add the sugar cube to a rocks glass. Douse with aromatic and orange bitters. Muddle until combined.

Add whiskey. Muddle/stir until most of the sugar is dissolved. This may take some time.

Add ice and stir until chilled.

Garnish with a maraschino cherry and an expressed orange swath.

Penicillin

Perhaps the most modern of our *True Classics*, legendary Australian bartender Sam Ross's creation layers smoky Islay Scotch on top of a gingery Whiskey Fix to make one of my favorite drinks of all time. I've riffed on it to create **Cupid's Chokehold** (page 150).

INGREDIENTS

2 ounces (60 ml) blended Scotch whisky

½ ounce (15 ml) ginger syrup (see page 25)

½ ounce (15 ml) honey syrup (see page 24)

½ ounce (15 ml) lemon juice, freshly squeezed

½ ounce (15 ml) Islay Scotch whisky

Candied ginger, to garnish (see page 27)

Lemon swath, to garnish (see page 27)

METHOD

Add the blended Scotch, ginger syrup, honey syrup, and lemon juice to a shaker.

Add ice and shake until chilled.

Double strain into an ice-filled rocks glass

Float with Islay Scotch (see page 31).

Garnish with candied ginger and an expressed lemon swath.

Piña Colada

My favorite "mocktail" as a kid was a virgin Piña Colada. I went on a cruise with my family when I was no older than 14 and probably had about 50 of the sweet, coconutty slushies during the trip. The alcoholic version has since become one of my favorite drinks to riff on—see the **Amarolada** (page 175), **Bit of Respite** (page 176), **Different Year** (page 169), and **Woah There Mambo** (page 99).

INGREDIENTS

2 ounces (60 ml) rum

1½ ounces (45 ml) cream of coconut

1½ ounces (45 ml) pineapple juice

½ ounce (15 ml) lime juice, freshly squeezed

Pineapple fronds, to garnish (page 28)

METHOD

Add the rum, cream of coconut, pineapple juice, and lime juice to a shaker.

Add ice and shake until chilled.

Dump (see page 31) into a chilled hurricane or wineglass.

Garnish with pineapple fronds and a cocktail umbrella.

Sazerac

This recipe for the unique, absinthe-laced New Orleans cocktail more closely follows the classic Sazerac spec than it does the modern one. **Tequila Me Elmo** (page 149) took inspiration from this classic.

INGREDIENTS

Absinthe, to rinse

2 ounces (60 ml) brandy

4 dashes Peychaud's bitters

1 dash aromatic bitters

¼ ounce (7.5 ml) demerara syrup (see page 23)

Lemon swath, to garnish (see page 27)

METHOD

Rinse a chilled snifter or Gibraltar glass with absinthe (see page 27).

Add the brandy, Peychaud's bitters, aromatic bitters, and demerara syrup to a mixing glass.

Add ice and stir until chilled and diluted, 15 to 20 seconds.

Strain into the prepared glass.

Garnish with an expressed lemon swath.

Scofflaw

The term *scofflaw* originated from a 1920s newspaper competition wherein readers were tasked to suggest names for people who broke the law by consuming or making alcohol during Prohibition. The clear winner was scofflaw: someone who scoffs at the law. Smart-ass scofflaws then raced to create a drink named after the new term, and this complex cocktail was born. The **10/10** (page 109) was influenced by the whiskey/dry vermouth combination in the Scofflaw.

INGREDIENTS

2 ounces (60 ml) rye whiskey

1 ounce (30 ml) dry vermouth

2 dashes orange bitters

½ ounce (15 ml) grenadine (see page 23)

¼ ounce (7.5 ml) lemon juice, freshly squeezed

Lemon swath, to garnish (see page 27)

METHOD

Add the rye whiskey, dry vermouth, orange bitters, grenadine, and lemon juice to a shaker.

Add ice and shake until chilled.

Double strain into a chilled coupe glass.

Garnish with an expressed lemon swath.

Whiskey Sour

A Sour must have an egg white to be called a Sour. If it doesn't, it is a fix cocktail. While whiskey, gin, and pisco may be the standards for this style of drink, you may use whatever spirit you like here. Each experiment will result in a brand-new cocktail. For the purposes of this recipe, we're using whiskey. Any egg white cocktail in this book, such as the **Alstonville Sour** (page 89) and the **Apple Pie Sour** (page 96), counts as a Sour riff.

INGREDIENTS

1½ ounces (45 ml) whiskey

¾ ounce (15 ml) lemon juice, freshly squeezed

¾ ounce (15 ml) demerara syrup (see page 23)

1 egg white

Aromatic or Peychaud's bitters, to garnish (see page 27)

METHOD

Add the whiskey, lemon juice, demerara syrup, and egg white to a shaker.

Dry shake until emulsified and frothy, about 15 seconds.

Add ice and shake until chilled.

Double strain into a chilled coupe glass. Let the froth settle for 1 to 2 minutes.

Garnish by adding drops of aromatic or Peychaud's bitters on the surface of the drink. Swirl a cocktail pick through the bitters to achieve the desired marbled effect.

Mine

—Hey, I Invented These!

The vast majority of the drinks I've made and tasted in the past have been invented by someone else—another talented drink-maker's creation. It didn't take me long, however, to start writing and formulating some of my own.

I mentioned earlier in this book that, as a child, I loved to cook. Not only that, I loved making up recipes on the fly. I had a few specialties as an eight-year-old, and almost all of them included copious amounts of food dye. Pink Muffins. Green Pancakes. Orange Red Velvet Birthday Cakes. You get the gist.

The older I got, the less fun my creations became and the more bored and annoyed I got with the energy and mess that seemed to go hand in hand with making food. I ditched my childhood dream of being on *Junior MasterChef Australia* and spent the remainder of my school years in a constant loop of being on movie sets, then returning to my rural town, egregiously cocky about having just been on a movie set. While I still act,

I'd like to think I've since overcome my conceited personality that used to overtake teen-me 24/7, if only just.

I only mention this because I truly believe that drink-making has forced me to abandon (at least some of) my arrogance. Food and drink have always occupied massive portions of my psyche, with visiting local restaurants and bars being my favorite activity to do while traveling. A fascination with flavors and how different people's taste buds have influenced the meals and drinks we now consider "classic" has been a constant joy throughout my life, something I hope I never lose.

It took me some time to know what different spirits and bottles taste like and how to blend their flavors in a pleasing manner, and there's still so much in the mixology world that I don't know. So, please, take these recipes, riff on them, make them better. For I'm not a genius. I'm not the be-all and end-all. I'm merely a boy.

Let's just go ahead and do it.

Lonely Valentine

● FRUITY   ▲ BITTER   ▲ TART

This drink, crafted on one of my TikTok livestreams, lives in the camp of cocktails that aren't exactly what they seem. The gorgeously pink, frothy, seemingly cutesy cocktail, with the sugared rim and bitters heart garnish, is anything but sweet and dainty. Once the drinker takes a sip, they are met with the bitter notes of the Campari and the savory taste of tequila.

The Lonely Valentine and **Cupid's Chokehold** (page 150) are sisters in action, vying to take down Valentine's Day once and for all. I'm Switzerland here; I don't have a horse in that race. I just know that both drinks are banging and you should have them in your mouth ASAP.

INGREDIENTS

¾ ounce (22.5 ml) tequila

¾ ounce (22.5 ml) Campari

¾ ounce (22.5 ml) grenadine (see page 23)

¾ ounce (22.5 ml) lemon juice, freshly squeezed

1 egg white

Aromatic or Peychaud's bitters, to garnish (see page 27)

METHOD

Add the tequila, Campari, grenadine, lemon juice, and egg white to a shaker.

Dry shake until emulsified and frothy, about 15 seconds.

Add ice and shake until chilled.

Double strain into a chilled coupe glass, half-rimmed with sugar (see page 28). Let the froth settle for 1 to 2 minutes.

Garnish by adding a drop of aromatic or Peychaud's bitters on the surface of the drink. Drag a cocktail pick through the bitters to form a heart.

Jaffa Kick

● FRUITY   ■ CHOCOLATEY   ▲ SPICY

This spicy chocolate orange in liquid form tickles the throat as it soothes the tongue with cocoa-coated citrus. This concoction was invented by my followers and me on a TikTok livestream, a result of brainstorming drink ideas with the viewers in the comments. Once the drink was made, a clever commenter said it must taste like a Jaffa Cake, a popular orange-chocolate biscuit (cookie) from England.

Deciding that that name didn't fully encapsulate the spiciness and savoriness of the cocktail, it was renamed the Jaffa Kick.

INGREDIENTS

1 ounce (30 ml) tequila

1 ounce (30 ml) orange liqueur

¾ ounce (22.5 ml) Averna amaro

¾ ounce (22.5 ml) cocoa bitters

½ teaspoon hot sauce

Orange swath, to garnish (see page 27)

METHOD

Add the tequila, orange liqueur, Averna amaro, cocoa bitters, and hot sauce to a mixing glass.

Add ice and stir until chilled and diluted, 15 to 20 seconds.

Strain into an ice-filled rocks glass.

Garnish with an expressed orange swath.

NOTES

• You're doing a heavy pour of bitters here, so use a quality one. I use Angostura Cocoa Bitters, but Fee Brothers' Aztec Chocolate Bitters are another great, slightly more complex option.

• The savory, tomato/vinegar nature of hot sauce can elevate cocktails and adds spice in a way that chili liqueur often can't. You may choose to leave it out of this drink, though it will lose a layer. My preferred universal hot sauces for this cocktail are Cholula or Tapatío, with Tabasco being a more savory, barbecue-y option.

Tapsalteerie

For years, whenever someone asked me what my favorite drink was—a common question people reach for upon hearing I do drinking for a living—my easy answer was a **Manhattan** (page 48). The simplicity of the drink and the apparent inability to mess it up lands it at the top of the food chain for me. Or drink chain, rather.

If I'm feeling talkative, though, I lead the inquirer through my own creation, the Tapsalteerie. It's a riff on Jeremy Oertel's Topsy Turvy, which is a riff on the aforementioned Manhattan, with more depth of flavor and more nuance, all the while transforming the boozy delight into a lighter, easier-to-down beverage.

This contender for my favorite cocktail of all time is designed for anyone who shares my same passion for making fortified wine the backbone of a cocktail rather than a backup dancer.

Tapsalteerie is the Scots' version of the phrase "topsy-turvy," meaning upside down. The whisky from their homeland subs in for the original's rye, bolstered by a heavier pour of coffee liqueur to create a cocktail that could warm the Highlands on a brisk winter evening.

INGREDIENTS

2 ounces (60 ml) sweet vermouth

1 ounce (30 ml) blended Scotch whisky

½ ounce (15 ml) coffee liqueur

1 dash cocoa bitters

Orange swath, to garnish (see page 27)

METHOD

Add the sweet vermouth, blended Scotch, coffee liqueur, and cocoa bitters to a mixing glass.

Add ice and stir until chilled and diluted, 15 to 20 seconds.

Strain into a chilled coupe glass.

Garnish with an expressed orange swath.

Hamilton Island Iced Tea

● FRUITY　　　　■ FIZZY　　　　▲ BITTER

This drink was born after I set out to reinvent the Long Island Iced Tea (LIIT), a feat I'm sure almost every mixologist has attempted. It's almost impossible to do without stepping on the tradition of the beverage. The very nature of the drink—which is made by sloshing *five* different spirits and liqueurs into a glass and masking that trash water with cola, lime, and simple syrup—is to get you wasted without tasting any alcohol. This approach, as unadmirable as it already is, doesn't even make any sense, considering the ABV of the drink is less than 20 percent, midrange at best. How do you make that fancy? How do you make it half-palatable? You add more alcohol.

That's right, this drink has *seven* different spirits and liqueurs and is stronger than a LIIT, by the numbers. The inclusion of the cola, citrus, and simple syrup makes this a definitive LIIT variation, albeit a much more upmarket one. The added Averna and Benedictine work to bring out the tastiest notes of the rest of the spirits and balance everything to make a drink that evolves stunningly. Also, Jarritos. Don't get me started on Jarritos. Liquid gold. Find some, please.

INGREDIENTS

1½ ounces (45 ml) Hamilton Island Iced Tea (HIIT) Mix (see *Method*)

⅓ ounce (10 ml) Averna amaro

¼ ounce (7.5 ml) Benedictine

⅓ ounce (10 ml) lemon juice, freshly squeezed

¼ ounce (7.5 ml) simple syrup (see page 23)

1½ ounces (45 ml) Jarritos Mexican Cola

Lemon swath, to garnish (see page 27)

METHOD

To make the HIIT Mix: Add equal parts (at least ½ ounce [15 ml] each) gin, vodka, funky rum, tequila, and orange liqueur to a container. (I used these brands, respectively: Tanqueray, Tito's, Hamilton Jamaican Pot Still Black, Espolòn Reposado, and Pierre Ferrand's Dry Curaçao.)

Leave for at least 2 hours before use.

To make the cocktail: Add the HIIT mix to a shaker. Dry shake to decant, 10 seconds.

Add Averna amaro, Benedictine, lemon juice, and simple syrup to shaker.

Add ice and shake until chilled.

Double strain into an ice-filled double rocks glass or highball glass.

Add the Mexican cola and stir to combine.

Garnish with an expressed lemon swath.

NOTE

If you want the best of the best, track down some Jarritos Mexican Cola. In my opinion, no other colas even come close to the flavor of Jarritos, and it's a defining factor of what separates this drink from a Long Island Iced Tea. In a pinch, you may use Mexican Coca-Cola.

Cuke of Lemonshire

● FRUITY   ▦ FIZZY   ▲ TART

The inception point of this cocktail is fairly blurry, as it was one of the first drinks I ever coined as my own. It's likely that I had a cucumber left over from the previous night's dinner and felt inclined to make a drink reminiscent of a fancy spa water.

    The gorgeous thing about this drink is that, by not muddling the cucumber, its essence slowly infuses the drink as it sits, complementing the botanicals of the gin and the elderflower brilliantly. The lemon brightens everything, resulting in a delightfully summery and refreshing cocktail.

INGREDIENTS

3 cucumber slices, halved

1½ ounces (45 ml) gin

½ ounce (15 ml) elderflower liqueur

¾ ounce (22.5 ml) lemon juice, freshly squeezed

3 ounces (90 ml) Sprite

2 ounces (60 ml) soda water

Cucumber slice, to garnish (see page 28)

Mint sprig, to garnish (see page 28)

METHOD

Add the cucumber slices and ice to a highball glass.

Add the gin, elderflower liqueur, and lemon juice to shaker.

Add ice and shake until chilled.

Strain into the prepared glass.

Top with Sprite and soda water. Stir to combine.

Garnish with a cucumber slice and a sprig of mint.

NOTES

- Sprite may be substituted with the drinker's preferred sweetened lemon-lime soda. Flavored sodas can tend to overpower a drink, so splitting it with soda water here allows the flavors of the base mixture to shine. Experiment with the ratio of lemon-lime soda to soda water to find your preferred blend.

- Slices of fresh, seasonal fruit may be added to this drink, along with the cucumber, to give the cocktail more of a summer punch vibe.

Dirty Shirley
OR FANCYPANTS

⬤ FRUITY   ▦ FIZZY   ▲ RICH

One of many cocktails I've curated for loved ones (**Aristaeus**, page 190; **Dad's Tea**, page 173; **Mum's Hum**, page 79; to name but a few), this recipe was written up for my Nan, my mum's mum. Her real name is Shirley, so when formulating a drink recipe inspired by her crafting an alcoholic version of the Shirley Temple felt like a no-brainer.

That meant thinking of what alcoholic ingredient to add to the already delicious combo of ginger ale and grenadine to improve it. While I feel like bourbon would be the most obvious choice, it was a jumping-off point for the final answer: Southern Comfort.

Southern Comfort was my late uncle Ross (Nan's only son)'s favorite liqueur, a sweet, fruity pour with a bourbon base. Ross, who was also my godfather, was the entertainer of the family. He dressed up and sung as Elvis Presley at his own 40th birthday party, just to make everyone else laugh. There's a very big chance his personality and energy influenced me, however subconsciously, to pursue my life of entertainment—the pursuit that has led me to where I am today.

The least I can do for him is to shoehorn his legacy into every step of that entertainment career. In that, here is my version of a "dirty" Shirley Temple.

INGREDIENTS

½ ounce (15 ml) grenadine (see page 23)

1½ ounces (45 ml) Southern Comfort

3 ounces (135 ml) ginger ale

2½ ounces (75 ml) soda water

Lime wedge, to garnish (see page 27)

METHOD

Add the grenadine to the bottom of a highball glass.

Add ice and the Southern Comfort, ginger ale, and soda water.

Stir until chilled and combined.

Garnish with a lime wedge.

NOTES

◆ Southern Comfort is a sweet, fruity liqueur that uses bourbon as a base. In a pinch, you may substitute bourbon or brandy for it, but the resulting drink will be drier.

◆ You can make your own ginger ale, though I never have. Canada Dry is a more than passable option, and it's what I've used since I began making drinks all those years ago.

Spins

● FRUITY　　　　■ FLORAL　　　　▲ TART

I've mentioned that I like to create drinks for loved ones. Well, one or two steps above that, it turns out, is writing a song about them and releasing it for the masses to listen to.

My longest-running boyfriend, now ex, who inspired two other drinks in this book (**Rosy Cheeks** on page 183 and **10/10** on page 109), gained that status in lightning speed.

On our second date, he gave me a tour of his Hoboken, New Jersey, college. I'd had a few drinks prior to our date, and we'd been gifted shots by the waiter who thought we were cute, so I was a bit worse for wear. We stumbled to his favorite place on campus, a bench overlooking the NYC skyline, sat down, and started to do kissing, only for me to realize I couldn't close my eyes without the whole world spinning. I was faced with two options: open my eyes and risk him opening his to see me staring back at him as we made out, or stop and admit my drunk state. I hesitantly opted for the latter and, the guy that he is, he was absolutely okay with it. So we just sat there, looking out at the Hudson River, as I tried my best to not blurt out that I already loved him.

The next morning, head aching, I wrote Spins, a song about that very date. A year later, the song was released and this floral cocktail was concocted to promote it.

INGREDIENTS

2 ounces (60 ml) white rum

1 ounce (30 ml) raspberry syrup (see page 24)

1 ounce (30 ml) lemon juice, freshly squeezed

4 drops rose water

Lemon swath, to garnish (see page 27)

METHOD

Add the white rum, raspberry syrup, lemon juice, and rose water to a shaker.

Add ice and shake until chilled.

Double strain into a chilled coupe glass.

Garnish with an expressed lemon swath.

NOTE

Rose water can be *extremely* potent, so be careful here. You can always add more. It may be omitted, but a layer of complexity will be lost.

Action Royale
OR GLORIFIED VODKA RED BULL

● FRUITY   ■ FLORAL   ▲ FIZZY

It just so happened that when Haleigh Hekking, my co-star in our short-lived Snapchat (yes, Snapchat) series, *Action Royale*, and I began brainstorming wrap gifts to give the cast and crew, I'd just gotten into jarring craft cocktails and gifting them to friends. Creating a cocktail recipe for the show and subsequently jarring 60 of them seemed like a tall task, but one that proved to be a pretty awesome present.

The idea for the drink came from the extremely odd fact (to me) that Red Bull had paid for some product placement in the show. This being the case, Red Bull was *everywhere* throughout the shoot. I'd come back to my trailer to a fridge full of the stuff every day, and craft services had cans upon cans on standby just in case one of us got a little sleepy. The liquid jet fuel in a can basically energized the entire show, so it just had to be part of the drink named after it.

I jarred the base and gave each of the cast and crew one jar and one can of Red Bull each, with a card detailing how to mix the two for the optimal drinking experience. Haleigh had some game-controller key chains made, on account of the show centering on an illegal video game gambling operation, so everyone got one of those as a garnish. If you, for whatever reason, don't have an *Action Royale* key chain, you can settle for a lime wedge here.

INGREDIENTS

1½ ounces (45 ml) vodka

¾ ounce (22.5 ml) elderflower liqueur

¾ ounce (22.5 ml) orange liqueur

2 dashes orange bitters

1 dash aromatic bitters

3½ ounces (105 ml) Red Bull

Lime wedge, to garnish (see page 27)

METHOD

Add the vodka, elderflower liqueur, orange liqueur, orange bitters, and aromatic bitters to an ice-filled highball glass.

Stir until chilled.

Top with Red Bull.

Garnish with a lime wedge.

NOTE

I suppose, while this drink is meant to symbolize a Glorified Vodka Red Bull, almost any energy drink or sweet soda could be used in its place here. A kombucha could be fun, even!

Mum's Hum
OR TICKLED PINK

● FRUITY ■ **FLORAL** ▲ FIZZY

This drink was crafted in celebration of my mum (who doesn't like to be called mother) on her 48th birthday.

One of the first drinks I regularly consumed after turning 18 in Australia was the classic Gin and Tonic. This story is vague in my memory, but I recollect ordering my mum her first G&T at a hotel bar, which seemed to spark her eventual love of all things gin. Mum's tastes have since expanded, but gin remained a backbone of her drinking catalog for quite a while.

Originally titled Tickled Pink, the name was changed to recognize mum's tendency, when slightly tipsy, to hum songs under her breath. Like taking your broken car to a mechanic only to have it work perfectly once you get there, no one has heard her do this since I renamed the drink, so Tickled Pink remains a subtitle.

Mum's Hum combines not one but *two* gins with flowers, fruit, citrus, and bubbles, all the hallmarks of a refreshing sipper, to form a gorgeously summery, tart, sweet highball that is sure to make you hum all the nursery rhymes and country ballads you can recall.

INGREDIENTS

1 ounce (30 ml) gin

1 ounce (30 ml) pink gin

¾ ounce (22.5 ml) elderflower liqueur

1 ounce (30 ml) raspberry syrup (see page 24)

¾ ounce (22.5 ml) lemon juice, freshly squeezed

2 ounces (60 ml) soda water

Lime wheel, to garnish (see page 27)

METHOD

Add the gin, pink gin, elderflower liqueur, raspberry syrup, and lemon juice to a shaker.

Add ice and shake until chilled.

Strain into an ice-filled highball glass.

Top with soda water.

Garnish with a lime wheel.

NOTE

This drink was originally made with Beefeater Pink Gin as the called-for pink gin. Since the cocktail's inception, that specific bottle has been tough to find in my locality. Other, less sweet pink gins exist and are more readily available, such as Salcombe's Rosé Sainte Marie Gin. Feel free to sub out the ingredient entirely for Pimm's No. 1, or just double the amount of regular gin.

Classy Boy

Another crowd-sourced concoction from a TikTok livestream, this drink takes the classic **Bramble** (page 40), flips it around, and makes it an egg white Sour. The name comes from my "Cocktail Name Game," where my TikTok followers make up cocktail names and I create a drink that suits that name.

Someone chucked Classy Boy at me and, immediately, my mind flew to English drinks. The Bramble is one of the most gorgeous cocktails to look at, all the while maintaining a royal air and classy flavor. Adding elderflower liqueur only adds to that regal feel. Throw in an egg white to add a velvety mouthfeel and thick froth, which is then doused with crème de mûre (a blackberry liqueur), and you've got one of the classiest boys I've ever tasted. Don't quote me on that.

This isn't a layered drink, per se. It's more of a "marbled" one. To create the desired effect, be gentle when pouring in the crème de mûre. When drinking, take one sip. You'll taste the bright gin, elderflower, and citrus notes. Then stir to combine everything and fully experience the sweet nature of the Classy Boy.

INGREDIENTS

1½ ounces (45 ml) gin

½ ounce (15 ml) elderflower liqueur

¾ ounce (22.5 ml) lemon juice, freshly squeezed

1 egg white

½ ounce (15 ml) crème de mûre (blackberry liqueur)

METHOD

Add the gin, elderflower liqueur, lemon juice, and egg white to a shaker.

Dry shake until emulsified, 15 seconds.

Add ice and shake until chilled.

Double strain into a chilled coupe glass. Let the froth settle for 1 to 2 minutes.

Gently pour crème de mûre into the drink.

Applewood Lager Co.

On an evening during the pandemic, I watched a video about the use of beer in cocktails. I brainstormed some ideas, and the combination of lager with apple juice and cinnamon came to mind. The autumnal notes play off the savory, hoppy beer in such a fun way, creating a flavor I'd never really tasted before.

If you're a fan of both apple cider and beer, this drink is a no-brainer. With its low ABV, it's also a phenomenal summer BBQ drink. You can be creative with serving this too. I've imagined making the base cocktail in a massive punch bowl and having guests at a party serve themselves one ladle's worth before grabbing a beer and mixing the two. You can easily multiply the bourbon, juice, and syrup by as many factors as you want, and the base-to-beer ratio is very forgiving.

INGREDIENTS

1 ounce (30 ml) bourbon

2½ ounces (75 ml) apple juice

½ ounce (15 ml) cinnamon syrup (see page 24)

3 ounces (90 ml) beer

Lemon wheel, to garnish (see page 27)

METHOD

Add the bourbon, apple juice, and cinnamon syrup to a shaker.

Add ice and shake until chilled.

Strain into an ice-filled highball glass.

Top with beer.

Garnish with a lemon wheel.

Serve alongside the remaining beer.

NOTES

• Fresh or bottled 100 percent real apple juice, not from concentrate, is best here.

• The beer in this drink could be anything from a commercially available blonde lager to a hoppy, fruity IPA. I would just steer clear of a dark, stout-like beer. If the drinker isn't partial to the flavor of beer, remove both the beer and the apple juice from the recipe and sub in 5½ ounces (165 ml) of hard apple cider to make the Applewood *Cider* Co.

You, Baby

● FRUITY   ■ HERBAL   ▲ TART

The celebration of my first birthday after moving to New York in 2022 consisted of multiple parties, one of which I held at my small studio apartment, filling it with way too many close friends. My position at this party was one of host/bartender, stationing myself at my home bar, mixing drinks for anyone who requested one. This may seem like a laborious way to spend my birthday evening, but I loved every second of it. I've always enjoyed hosting, so being able to impress my friends solely by allowing them to imbibe in my creations was a pure joy.

Later on in the night, one of my then boyfriend's dear friends, Sofie, asked for a drink. As I had with the other guests who had made the same request, I asked her what she liked. She sultrily replied, "You, Baby," and my mind ran wild in multiple ways. We'll be focusing on the cocktail way. The resulting spec that has landed in this book was my very first attempt at the You, Baby, a stat I'm always proud of.

Almost a riff on a Martinez with adjusted ratios and added citrus, the drink I handed Sofie seemed to surprise and delight her. I took a sip from her hands and the same emotions overtook me. The story behind a cocktail always makes a drink more interesting, and this is one of my favorites.

INGREDIENTS

1¼ ounces (37.5 ml) gin

1¼ ounces (37.5 ml) sweet vermouth

⅔ ounce (20 ml) maraschino liqueur

⅓ ounce (10 ml) lemon juice, freshly squeezed

Lemon swath, to garnish (see page 27)

Maraschino cherry, to garnish (see page 28)

METHOD

Add the gin, sweet vermouth, maraschino liqueur, and lemon juice to a shaker.

Add ice and shake until chilled.

Double strain into a chilled coupe glass.

Garnish with an expressed lemon swath and/or a maraschino cherry.

Improved Fluff

● FRUITY   ▦ FUNKY   ▲ BITTER

The term *improved* began appearing in cocktail manuals and bar guides in the late 1800s, signaling a trend toward "enhancing" the classics with additional ingredients. I've always thought that marketing a cocktail as an "improved" version of a preexisting beverage screamed pretentious mixologist. After all, taste is subjective, right? I held that opinion until I tried the Improved Whiskey Cocktail. The original is great and classic, but the complexity the additional ingredients and different measures added made for a stunning drink.

My first foray into the "improved" world came when I tasted Fanny Chu's Tropical Fluff and thought it was, while delicious, much too sweet for my taste. I adjusted the ratios and replaced Aperol with the more bracing Campari to create what *I* think is a delectable mouthful.

INGREDIENTS

1 ounce (30 ml) funky rum (see *Notes*)

¾ ounce (22.5 ml) crème de banane

½ ounce (15 ml) Campari

1½ ounces (45 ml) pineapple juice

¾ ounce (22.5 ml) orange juice

½ ounce (15 ml) grapefruit juice

Pineapple fronds, to garnish (see page 28)

METHOD

Add the rum, crème de banane, Campari, pineapple juice, orange juice, and grapefruit juice to a shaker.

Dry shake until frothy.

Add ice and shake until chilled.

Double strain into an ice-filled rocks glass.

Garnish with pineapple fronds.

NOTES

◆ Shoot for one of the funkiest aged Caribbean rums you can find here (Hamilton Jamaican Pot Still Black and Angostura 1919 are personal standouts).

◆ Be sure to use freshly squeezed or 100 percent real orange and grapefruit juice here, not from concentrate, or you risk an unbalanced cocktail.

Million Follower Cocktail

● FRUITY　　　■ FUNKY　　　▲ **RICH**

Rum and sweet vermouth may not be a common pairing, but they go together *splendidly*. Here I use them in a drink I created to commemorate my TikTok account reaching a million followers, riffing on the existing Million Dollar Cocktail.

While you'd expect the intense flavors of the pineapple, rum, and vermouth to battle, they actually combine with the egg white to make quite a light, gentle drink. I mentioned in this drink's dedicated TikTok that it tastes how the fluffy pink froth that settles on the top of the cocktail looks. It tastes pretty. And that's more than I need.

INGREDIENTS

1½ ounces (45 ml) white rum

¾ ounce (22.5 ml) sweet vermouth

½ ounce (15 ml) pineapple juice

1 teaspoon grenadine (see page 23)

1 egg white

Aromatic or Peychaud's bitters, to garnish (see page 27)

METHOD

Add the rum, sweet vermouth, pineapple juice, grenadine, and egg white to a shaker.

Dry shake until emulsified and frothy, about 15 seconds.

Add ice and shake until chilled.

Double strain into a chilled coupe glass. Let the froth settle for 1 to 2 minutes.

Garnish by adding drops of aromatic or Peychaud's bitters on the surface of the drink. Swirl a cocktail pick through the bitters to achieve the desired marbled effect.

Alstonville Sour

Any drink where I get to layer a colored liquid on top of a differently colored liquid to create a stark contrast is a drink I'm going to like making. It's a bonus if it tastes good too.

The New York Sour is essentially a regular Whiskey Fix (whiskey, lemon, sugar) with a red wine float. The Greenwich Sour is a New York Sour with an egg white added to achieve the quintessentially frothy nature of a modern **Whiskey Sour** (page 60) while maintaining the added complexity of a red wine float.

That leads me to the Alstonville Sour, named after my childhood hometown. It doesn't have anything to do with the place itself, it's just what a Greenwich Sour would be if I had invented it in the first place. Funky, fruity tawny port replaces the red wine, and cinnamon syrup takes the simple syrup's spot to create an end product that tastes like if raisins got their juice back.

INGREDIENTS

1½ ounces (45 ml) bourbon

¾ ounce (22.5 ml) lemon juice, freshly squeezed

¾ ounce (22.5 ml) cinnamon syrup (see page 24)

1 egg white

1 ounce (30 ml) tawny port

METHOD

Add the bourbon, lemon juice, cinnamon syrup, and egg white to a shaker.

Dry shake until emulsified and frothy, about 15 seconds.

Add ice and shake until chilled.

Double strain into an ice-filled rocks glass.

Float with tawny port (see page 31).

NOTE

Port, much like vermouth, is a fortified wine. Where vermouth is usually French or Italian, port must originate in Portugal. It's funky when well aged, and funk lends itself to this cocktail phenomenally. When formulating this recipe, I used W&J Graham's 20 Year Tawny Port, but any similarly aged tawny should work here. Oloroso or Amontillado sherry may be used as a substitute.

Tai One On

● FRUITY   ■ NUTTY   ▲ FIZZY

Inspired by Jonathan Pogash's Brooklyn Tai, which is already one of my faves, this drink maintains the tropical vibe of a **Mai Tai** (page 47), with the rum and the orgeat being the main players here, while the lager serves as a welcome savory backboard that allows every single flavor to shine. I'm a *big* fan of this one. If you like it too, try the **Applewood Lager Co.** (page 82).

Bonus: "Tie one on" is an abbreviation of an old English expression, "tie the bun on." In the 1870s, a test to prove you were sober was to walk with a bun on your head. If you were drunk it would fall off unless you "tied the bun on" to your head to pass the test. I *love* stuff like that.

INGREDIENTS

1½ ounces (45 ml) rum

2 dashes aromatic bitters

¾ ounce (22.5 ml) orgeat (see page 24)

½ ounce (15 ml) orange juice

¼ ounce (7.5 ml) lime juice, freshly squeezed

3 ounces (90 ml) beer

Lime wheel, to garnish (see page 27)

METHOD

Add the rum, aromatic bitters, orgeat, orange juice, and lime juice to a shaker.

Add ice and shake until chilled.

Strain into an ice-filled highball glass.

Top with beer.

Garnish with a lime wheel.

NOTES

- I prefer a rum on the tamer side here. Hamilton's Demerara Rum or a lighter Puerto Rican style would both work great.

- Be sure to use freshly squeezed or 100 percent real orange juice here, not from concentrate, or you risk an unbalanced cocktail.

- The beer in this drink could be anything from a commercially available blonde lager to a hoppy, kooky IPA. I would just steer clear of a dark, stout-like beer.

Top Hat and a Hat Tan

● FRUITY   ■ NUTTY   ▲ TART

This slightly tropical version of the classic **Bramble** (page 40) is a complex, fruity delight that is sure to make a sweaty forehead on a summer's day disappear in seconds. Sloe gin, a somewhat unknown ingredient in the Americas, serves as an earthy companion to the crisp apple brandy and lightly funky white rum to allow this drink to claw its way out of the realm of being too cloying and too sweet.

Pairing citrus with apple brandy always gives any drink the delicious tasting note of hard apple cider. In this cocktail, orgeat, an almond syrup, turns that note into one of a delicious home-baked apple crumble. The berry syrup finally poured over the top of the crushed ice, a nod to the Bramble, brings this toasty dessert together with the earthy, funky base to create something pretty dang special. Slam a few back and stop sweating. You look gross!

INGREDIENTS

1 ounce (30 ml) sloe gin

1 ounce (30 ml) apple brandy

¾ ounce (22.5 ml) white rum

½ ounce (15 ml) lemon juice, freshly squeezed

½ ounce (15 ml) orgeat (see page 24)

½ ounce (15 ml) berry syrup (see page 24)

Pineapple fronds, to garnish (see page 28)

METHOD

Half-fill a double rocks glass with crushed ice.

Add the sloe gin, apple brandy, white rum, lemon juice, and orgeat to a shaker.

Add ice to the shaker and shake until chilled.

Strain into prepared glass.

Top with crushed ice.

Pour berry syrup over drink.

Garnish with pineapple fronds.

NOTES

• Sloe gin is gin infused with sloes, naturally. Sloes are a relative of plums, with a deep purple color and a *super* earthy, rooty taste resulting in a gin that isn't nearly as sweet as you might expect. There are plenty of great sloe gins on the market—Elephant, Plymouth, and Hayman's, to name but a few. There is no substitute.

• Any berry syrup can be used here! They all bring something different but all taste great, so just pick your favorite.

Prime Minister

● FRUITY　　　　■ RICH　　　　▲ FLORAL

Let me vent, please, for but a second.

The desire to get drunk without tasting the alcohol (a phenomenon I'm dubbing the Long Island Iced Tea effect) is problematic and isn't talked about enough. I can't *stand* when people say, "This drink is so strong but so smooth, woahhhhhh." Those people seem to think that "tasting liquor" means feeling a burn in the back of your throat, and if that sensation doesn't occur, the drink is perfect. In reality, no cocktail, regardless of ABV, when made well and balanced correctly, should "burn." If a drink does "burn," not only is it not a good cocktail, but that doesn't even necessarily indicate that it's highly potent. It could just be made poorly.

Crafting boozy cocktails that don't taste boozy is an art form. Case in point: The delectable Prime Minister is made entirely of alcoholic ingredients (as are most other stirred cocktails), but the drink is "smooth," using ingredients with a higher sugar content to balance out the stronger ones. It's a well-made drink and it's tasty as a result.

To summarize, I wish people would stop drinking fistfuls of alcohol covered up with fruit juice or soda, with the intention of just getting wasted. You're embarrassing yourself. Rant over. Cheers!

INGREDIENTS

1½ ounces (45 ml)
  white rum

1½ ounces (45 ml)
  blanc vermouth

¼ ounce (7.5 ml)
  crème de banane

¼ ounce (7.5 ml)
  crème de mûre
  (blackberry liqueur)

Lemon swath, to garnish
  (see page 27)

METHOD

Add the white rum, blanc vermouth, crème de banane, and crème de mûre to a mixing glass.

Add ice and stir until chilled and diluted, 15 to 20 seconds.

Strain into a chilled coupe glass.

Garnish with an expressed lemon swath.

Lazy Lucifer

● FRUITY   ■ TART   ▲ FIZZY

This tasty little highball number is an improved version of one of the first cocktails I ever crafted that used grenadine, the bright red sugar water, purely so the name would make sense. I've since come to my senses and now prioritize taste over looks or the matching of a clever name to a cocktail at the sacrifice of well-balanced flavors. And that's growth.

Substituting a homemade strawberry syrup for the artificial trash that is premade grenadine allows the drink to maintain its red glow while adding a summery, naturally sweet note. Earthy sloe gin and bittersweet orange liqueur help create a concentrated, cordial-esque substance that, when watered down with soda water, becomes a cocktail one could just as quickly guzzle under the blazing sun as they could sip in front of a roaring fire. In hell, perhaps?

Speaking of, the name for the drink is an homage to the many cocktails named after the devil purely because they're red. I believe that practice is lazy and silly, so it's only natural I continue the sloppy tradition.

INGREDIENTS

1¼ ounces (37.5 ml)
  sloe gin

1¼ ounces (37.5 ml)
  orange liqueur

½ ounce (15 ml)
  strawberry syrup
  (see page 24)

½ ounce (15 ml) lemon
  juice, freshly squeezed

2 ounces (60 ml)
  soda water

Lime wheel, to garnish
  (see page 27)

METHOD

Add the sloe gin, orange liqueur, strawberry syrup, and lemon juice to a shaker.

Add ice and shake until chilled.

Strain into an ice-filled highball glass.

Top with soda water.

Garnish with a lime wheel.

NOTE

There are plenty of great sloe-infused gins on the market. Elephant, Plymouth, and Hayman's are my faves. There are no proper substitutes.

Apple Pie Sour

● FRUITY　　　　■ RICH　　　　▲ TART

My origin of this drink is fairly blurry, as it was one of the first drinks I ever coined as my own. It's likely that I felt inclined to make a cocktail that smelled and tasted like apple pie in a glass. And not to toot myself, but I succeeded.

I do remember originally trying to shoehorn apple juice into this recipe early on. But no matter how little of it was used, it always overpowered and watered down the drink. The cinnamon and citrus were lost and, I was left with bland, frothy apple nectar. Substituting the apple brandy for the juice was a game changer. The combination of apple brandy, citrus, and cinnamon makes this one taste exactly like the filling of an apple pie, and that's just nice.

INGREDIENTS

1½ ounces (45 ml) apple brandy

¾ ounce (22.5 ml) cinnamon whiskey

¾ ounce (22.5 ml) lemon juice, freshly squeezed

½ ounce (15 ml) cinnamon syrup (see page 24)

1 egg white

Freshly grated cinnamon (see page 28)

METHOD

Add the apple brandy, cinnamon whiskey, lemon juice, cinnamon syrup, and egg white to a shaker.

Dry shake until emulsified and frothy, about 15 seconds.

Add ice and shake until chilled.

Double strain into a chilled coupe glass. Let the froth settle for 1 to 2 minutes.

Garnish with freshly grated cinnamon.

NOTE

While you may hear the term *cinnamon whiskey* and immediately picture the liquid cinnamon icing that is Fireball, there are a few more organic, tastier, lovely bottles out there that should be put above it in every instance. I've used Clear Water's ScandaLust Cinnamon Whiskey for a while now. Its baking spice and raisiny notes, on top of the potent cinnamon nose and flavor, do wonders in making this drink feel as apple pie-y as possible. If you must use Fireball, remove the cinnamon syrup from the recipe.

Woah There Mambo

● FRUITY   ▦ SMOKY   ▲ **SPICY**

I honestly can't get enough of riffs on the classic **Piña Colada** (page 57). The drink is a canvas on which to add anything that might come close to complementing coconut and pineapple, which turns out to be a lot. Case in point, Woah There Mambo.

Adding spice in the form of jalapeño to Mark Hubbard's Hey Mambo, an already deliciously smoky and complex cocktail, takes it one more level up to create a throat-tickling, mature Piña Colada. Imagine a poolside speakeasy in an all-inclusive, adults-only resort—this would be their featured cocktail.

INGREDIENTS

1 ounce (30 ml) Campari

½ ounce (15 ml) mezcal

½ ounce (15 ml) tequila

1½ ounces (45 ml) pineapple juice

1½ ounces (45 ml) cream of coconut

¾ ounce (22.5 ml) lime juice, freshly squeezed

½ ounce (15 ml) jalapeño syrup (see page 25)

Pineapple fronds, to garnish (see page 28)

METHOD

Add the Campari, mezcal, tequila, pineapple juice, cream of coconut, lime juice, and jalapeño syrup to a shaker.

Add ice and shake until chilled.

Dump (see page 31) into a chilled hurricane or wineglass.

Garnish with pineapple fronds and a cocktail umbrella.

Gabe's Blueberry Cosmopolitan

● FRUITY ▬ TART ▲ RICH

I'll be straight honest with you; I've never liked Cosmopolitans. They're always strangely bland and watery, with the most prominent tasting notes coming from the alcohol burn of the vodka. So I was skeptical when my friend and fellow TikToker Gabe Escobar (@gabesco) DMed me a drink recipe at the beginning of my TikTok-tail renaissance that had the word Cosmopolitan in it. But Gabe swore by this recipe, and I'm a brilliant friend, and I like to drink, so what's the harm?

Upon trying it for the first time, in a TikTok video comparing it to the original Cosmo, all my hesitance faded. The sweetness of the blueberry jam completely rounds out the cocktail and lifts all the prominent, complementary flavors of the other ingredients. It wasn't just a faintly cranberry-ish vodka cocktail; it was something in a domain all its own. Gabe has really done something else here.

This is a silky, delicious, sweet, tart cocktail that I'm always more than tempted to suggest whenever anyone asks me for a Cosmopolitan, right after cringing.

INGREDIENTS

1 ounce (30 ml) vodka

1 ounce (30 ml) orange liqueur

1 ounce (30 ml) cranberry juice

½ ounce (15 ml) lemon juice, freshly squeezed

1 tablespoon blueberry jam

Blueberries, to garnish

Lemon swath, to garnish (see page 27)

METHOD

Add the vodka, orange liqueur, cranberry juice, lemon juice, and blueberry jam to a shaker.

Dry shake until emulsified, 15 seconds.

Add ice and shake until chilled.

Double strain into a chilled coupe glass.

Garnish with a cocktail pick of blueberries and an expressed lemon swath.

NOTES

• Ensure you get 100 percent cranberry juice, not cranberry cocktail or cran-apple juice. This is a surprisingly common mistake.

• As good blueberry jam tends to jam up a cocktail shaker (pun intended), you may substitute ½ ounce (15 ml) of blueberry syrup (see page 24).

Lemony Trick-It

● FRUITY   ■ TART   ▲ RICH

Reinventing the wheel is famously difficult. I mean, there's a whole phrase about it that starts with "don't." Reinventing Norman Jay Hobday's Lemon Drop doesn't have a phrase, so I think we're safe there.

The original is bracingly tart, sweet, and weirdly bland otherwise (vodka and simple syrup will do that). Brandy enters the frame here, joined by the tiniest skosh of overproof rum and honey, to make the Lemony Trick-It not only a drink with a fantastic name but a drink with a fantastic taste.

INGREDIENTS

1¾ ounces (52.5 ml) brandy

½ ounce (15 ml) orange liqueur

¼ ounce (7.5 ml) overproof rum

1 ounce (30 ml) lemon juice, freshly squeezed

¾ ounce (22.5 ml) honey syrup (see page 24)

Lemon swath, to garnish (see page 27)

METHOD

Add the brandy, orange liqueur, overproof rum, lemon juice, and honey syrup to a shaker.

Add ice and shake until chilled.

Double strain into a chilled coupe glass, half-rimmed with sugar (see page 28).

Garnish with an expressed lemon swath.

NOTE

The term *overproof* in any such spirit means it has a higher alcohol content than the standard. My go-to overproof rum is Wray & Nephew 126 Proof.

B2P2

I have a theory that no one actually likes sparkling wine. I think one day it was decided that the pop of a cork should mark celebration and someone said, "Hey, great idea! Does what's in the popped bottle taste nice?" which was answered by "Stop asking so many questions!" and now it's now.

The B2P2 was inspired by my ever-present desire for people who don't like sparkling wine to stop drinking glasses of the stuff just because they feel like they must.

The B2C2 is my go-to New Year's Eve drink. It's bubbly and refreshing while also boozy enough to get the party going. This riff uses grapefruit (pamplemousse) liqueur instead of orange (Cointreau) liqueur, and subs out the aforementioned champagne for prosecco, or really any sparkling wine, to form two Ps, instead of two Cs.

Be careful with these—one too many might make you miss midnight.

INGREDIENTS

1½ ounces (45 ml) brandy

1½ ounces (45 ml) Benedictine

1½ ounces (45 ml) grapefruit liqueur

1½ ounces (45 ml) sparkling wine

Lemon swath, to garnish (see page 27)

Maraschino cherry, to garnish (see page 28)

METHOD

Add the brandy, Benedictine, and grapefruit liqueur to a mixing glass.

Add ice and stir until chilled and diluted, 15 to 20 seconds.

Strain into a chilled champagne flute.

Top with sparkling wine.

Garnish with an expressed lemon swath and drop a maraschino cherry straight to the bottom of the glass.

NOTES

- For grapefruit liqueur, I like Giffard's Crème de Pample-mousse. You can substitute orange liqueur here, along with Champagne for the sparkling wine, to make a B2C2.

- You may use any sparkling wine/prosecco. Using the more expensive champagne is not necessary, but a sparkling rosé could be nice! La Marca Prosecco is a great value option.

Lonely Last Call

● HERBAL　　　■ BITTER　　　▲ FRUITY

I've never been a huge fan of the classically riffed-upon cocktail the Last Word, which is why it doesn't appear in this book. Not only do I find it to be a bit too bracing and sour, but the remaining flavors in a Last Word never pop as much as I'd like. I have a theory that no one actually likes the drink, which is possibly the reason behind almost every drink-maker in the world having a custom variation they prefer over it. Perhaps it's an incorrect opinion, but this is my book. Deal with it.

Traditionally based on gin, this riff on the classic substitutes the clear spirit with a dark one, bourbon. It removes the lime juice and replaces it with a slightly unusual method that I don't believe I've seen too much of outside the confines of my apartment: stirring with citrus peels. Doing so here not only removes the need for an expressed citrus swath garnish but also permeates the entire drink with the bitter oils from the orange, lemon, and lime, allowing the bitter flavor to complement the slightly sweet cocktail. Maraschino liqueur and Green Chartreuse are added to bring this one into the world of Last Word riffs, with the former also providing a deep, syrupy, cherry note.

The name for this drink came from a TikTok livestream comment. I stuck "Lonely Last Call" in my notebook and swore I'd come back to it. I'm very glad I did.

INGREDIENTS

1½ ounces (45 ml) bourbon

1 ounce (30 ml) Green Chartreuse

1 ounce (30 ml) maraschino liqueur

2 lemon swaths

2 lime swaths

2 orange swaths

Maraschino cherry, to garnish (see page 28)

METHOD

Add the bourbon, Green Chartreuse, and maraschino liqueur to a mixing glass.

Express citrus swath oils (see page 27) into mixing glass and add the swaths in.

Add ice and stir until chilled and diluted, 15 to 20 seconds.

Strain into a chilled coupe glass.

Garnish with a maraschino cherry.

NOTES

◆ Chartreuse comes in two colors: green and yellow. I've personally never stocked Yellow Chartreuse, as it is simply a meeker, sweeter version of Green Chartreuse, a powerful, bitter, peppery, herbaceous liqueur. The original Chartreuse has become difficult to find in recent years, so green herbal substitutes like Faccia Brutto Centerbe or Dolin Génépy le Chamois Liqueur may prove to be the only option.

◆ *Swath* is just a fancy name for a citrus peel. For this drink, you'll use two swaths from each citrus, so peel two vertical lengths of each fruit using a vegetable peeler.

London Fog

● HERBAL   ■ FLORAL   ▲ CREAMY

An homage to the classic milky tea traditionally enjoyed in the morning time, this boozy version riffs on the **Irish Coffee** (page 46), with a layer of thick cream lying peacefully on top of the honeyed tea cocktail.

Crafting a drink from scratch can call for a variety of methods. One of my favorites is to think of a cocktail name that doesn't exist and try to create a beverage for the title on the fly. The London Fog always sounded to me like a pretentious, posh cocktail you'd find on the menu of a rooftop bar in Kensington, so I ran with that idea.

Instead of using a classic latte recipe (Earl Grey tea, milk, and honey, served hot and garnished with lavender), which resulted in a drink that was too harsh, as is normally the case when one heats up gin, I decided to infuse the gin and serve this cold.

INGREDIENTS

2 ounces (60 ml) Earl Grey–infused gin (see *Method*)

1 dash lavender bitters

1 ounce (30 ml) honey syrup (see page 24)

1 dash vanilla extract

2 ounces (60 ml) heavy cream

2 dashes lavender bitters

2 dashes vanilla extract

METHOD

To make the Earl Grey–infused gin: Add 1 Earl Grey tea bag per every 4 ounces gin to a jar.

Cover and leave for 2 hours before removing tea bag and using.

To make the cocktail: Add 2 ounces of the Earl Grey–infused gin, 1 dash lavender bitters, honey syrup, and 1 dash vanilla to a mixing glass.

Add ice and stir until chilled and diluted, 15 to 20 seconds.

Strain into a chilled coupe glass.

Add the heavy cream, 2 dashes lavender bitters, and 2 dashes vanilla to a shaker. Stir to combine.

Float drink with cream mixture (see page 31).

NOTES

- Infusing may sound like a daunting task, but it's simply about time and patience. When infused alcohol is used in a complementary scenario, a drink can be elevated to incredible heights.

- Use high-quality 100 percent vanilla extract, not vanilla essence.

- Heavy cream is called for in this drink, as its density helps it float on top of the cocktail. Half-and-half or a plant-based alternative may work, but it might require some slight whipping.

H Woo Sour

● HERBAL   ■ FLORAL   ▲ TART

My dear friend and culinary TikTok phenom, H Woo Lee, is one of my favorite creators on the internet. His cooking videos are second to none, and his dishes are truly mouthwatering. So when he commented on one of my videos in January 2022, asking for a yuzu-based cocktail, I had to say yes. We've since hung out, a day which was fueled by good food and complex cocktails, as you can imagine.

PS: Love you, H Woo. Text me x

INGREDIENTS

1 ounce (30 ml) nama (unpasteurized) sake

1 ounce (30 ml) Benedictine

½ ounce (15 ml) yuzu juice

¼ ounce (7.5 ml) lemon juice, freshly squeezed

1 egg white

Freshly grated nutmeg, to garnish (see page 28)

Ground Szechuan peppercorns, to garnish (see *Notes*)

METHOD

Add the nama sake, Benedictine, yuzu juice, lemon juice, and egg white to a shaker.

Dry shake until emulsified, 15 seconds.

Add ice and shake until chilled.

Double strain into a chilled coupe glass. Let the froth settle for 1 to 2 minutes.

Garnish with freshly grated nutmeg or ground Szechuan peppercorns.

NOTES

♦ While also referred to as Japanese rice wine, sake's brewing process is actually more akin to that of beer. That being said, its varietals are as vast as wine, and each serves a different purpose. In my research, I've found that nama (unpasteurized) sake lends itself to most mixology the best, as it has that stunning, funky sake flavor you're likely searching for without overpowering the cocktail or disappearing into the drink.

♦ Yuzu is an east Asian citrus fruit that I've always described as tasting how a mandarin orange smells, whatever that may mean to you. It's much less sour than a lemon or a lime and much more aromatic. If you struggle to find fresh yuzu, high-quality bottled juice works as well, or you may substitute fresh lemon juice for it with the knowledge that the flavor will differ.

♦ Garnishing this drink with ground Szechuan peppercorns is completely unnecessary and extra, but the tingling, mouth-numbing sensation the spice causes is incredible and may be worth seeking out. For bonus points, lightly toast the peppercorns in a dry pan before grinding for added complexity.

10/10

● HERBAL · · · · · · ⊞ FRUITY · · · · · · ▲ **RICH**

The incredible afternoon that resulted in the making of this cocktail will forever be known as 10/10 to me and my then boyfriend, Jackson. It wasn't the 10th of October but rather our 10th date; an evening of cooking, drink-making, and dancing—just like in the movies!

After testing various **Scofflaw** (page 59) recipes that evening, I decided (as I tend to do) to try to create a new cocktail. Using the open bottle of dry vermouth, the notion of pairing it with rye whiskey (inspired by the Scofflaw testing), and my recent interest in experimenting with the syrup inside a jar of Luxardo maraschino cherries as my inspiration, I started to do stirring.

It's fairly rare for a cocktail to come out perfectly after the first test. Ratios often need to be adjusted to find the perfect balance. This was one of those rare times where Jackson and I both loved this first spec. It is complex, sweet, bitter, herbal, and spicy with a long, winding evolution. A truly unique, classy drink, reminiscent of a Brooklyn. Truly 10/10. ;)

INGREDIENTS

1 ounce (30 ml) rye whiskey

1 ounce (30 ml) dry vermouth

1 ounce (30 ml) Green Chartreuse

½ ounce (15 ml) maraschino cherry syrup (see *Notes*)

Lemon swath (see page 27)

METHOD

Add the rye, dry vermouth, Green Chartreuse, and maraschino cherry syrup to a mixing glass.

Add ice and stir until chilled and diluted, 15 to 20 seconds.

Strain into a chilled coupe glass.

Garnish with an expressed lemon swath.

NOTES

• The original Green Chartreuse has become difficult to find in recent years, so green herbal substitutes like Faccia Brutto Centerbe or Dolin Génépy le Chamois Liqueur have become adequate replacements.

• For clarity, when I say maraschino cherry syrup, I am talking about the literal syrup in a jar of maraschino cherries, NOT maraschino liqueur. Maraschino cherries have been a mainstay cocktail garnish for more years than I can count, but the syrupy, concentrated, cherry-flavored syrup they are jarred in is often overlooked and thrown out once the cherries have run their course. Using this liquid brings a rich cherry undertone and gorgeous deep purple hue to a cocktail. Ensure a proper jar of Luxardo maraschino cherries is used, not the bright red stuff you find on ice cream sundaes.

Philip

● HERBAL   ■ FRUITY   ▲ FUNKY

If you haven't yet met Philip, let me introduce you. He's bright, he's colorful, he's five foot two (ladieeeees). Oh, and he's a lamp. But he's hoping you can look past that.

The original Philip was purchased on Facebook Marketplace for a crisp $15. He was fitted with a soul (a Philips Hue light bulb, hence the name) placed behind my first DrinkTok video, and he's been there ever since, giving off both purple light and impeccable vibes.

Unfortunately, limited space meant he had to be thrown away following my move to a new apartment in 2023. The image of him being left by a dumpster sent the internet into a frenzy, so this color-changing riff on the **Martini** (page 50) was concocted in his memory. Months later, in my first Manhattan apartment, a replacement lamp was bought to house Philip's light bulb soul, to rapturous relief. Now, he's here to stay. We hope.

To Philip!

INGREDIENTS

2 ounces (60 ml) butterfly pea flower gin

1 ounce (30 ml) umeshu plum liqueur

2 dashes orange bitters

Lemon swath, to garnish (see page 27)

METHOD

Add the gin, plum liqueur, and orange bitters to a mixing glass.

Add ice and stir until chilled and diluted, 15 to 20 seconds.

Strain into a chilled coupe glass.

Garnish with an expressed lemon swath.

NOTES

• Butterfly pea flower gin is purely for effect here, as it makes the drink change color when the acidic liqueur is added. If that's less important to you, use whatever gin you like. If you want to be traditional, Empress 1908 is the standard bottle.

• Most vermouths will work in place of the plum liqueur here, especially a blanc vermouth. If you want to procure a bottle of umeshu (try your best, it's delicious), Choya is my preferred brand.

• The original version of this drink used peach bitters, but the orange variety works just as well and is more of a bar staple.

Attaché

● HERBAL   ■ FRUITY   ▲ RICH

Vermouth is gaining in popularity as a simple, lower ABV cocktail base. In this riff on the classic Diplomat, the Attaché showcases two vermouths, both bolstered by rooty, herbal Benedictine. Balanced out by a measly dash of aromatic bitters, this drink is one I always annoy bartenders with by asking them to make it for me because I've run out of vermouth at home.

INGREDIENTS

2 ounces (60 ml) blanc vermouth

1 ounce (30 ml) sweet vermouth

½ ounce (15 ml) Benedictine

1 dash aromatic bitters

Orange swath, to garnish (see page 27)

Maraschino cherry, to garnish (see page 28)

METHOD

Add the blanc vermouth, sweet vermouth, Benedictine, and aromatic bitters to a mixing glass.

Add ice and stir until chilled and diluted, 15 to 20 seconds.

Strain into a chilled coupe glass.

Garnish with an expressed orange swath and a maraschino cherry.

Singin' in the Rain

● HERBAL   ▨ FRUITY   ▲ TART

Absinthe is a divisive flavor, much like its flavor buddy, black licorice. It can also be wonderfully bracing, and when used in balanced scenarios, such as is done here, combining it with sweet and sour elements like the pineapple, sugar, and lime in this drink, the harsh notes are hidden and the mellow, smooth, aniseed-y ones remain. Add tequila to the mix and this cocktail goes down as fast as its predecessor's name (Hole in the Cup) implies.

If you want to explore absinthe further, do try the **Sazerac** (page 58) and the **Tequila Me Elmo** (page 149), both of which use the concentrated liqueur as a rinse on the glass prior to serving.

INGREDIENTS

1½ ounces (45 ml) tequila

¼ ounce (7.5 ml) absinthe

1 ounce (30 ml) pineapple juice

¾ ounce (22.5 ml) simple syrup (see page 23)

½ ounce (15 ml) lime juice, freshly squeezed

Lime wheel, to garnish (see page 27)

Cucumber slice, to garnish (see page 28)

METHOD

Add the tequila, absinthe, pineapple juice, simple syrup, and lime juice to a shaker.

Add ice and shake until chilled.

Double strain into a chilled coupe glass.

Garnish with a lime wheel or cucumber slice.

NOTE

I think almost all absinthes taste alike. Get either a small bottle or one that looks pretty, for a little lasts a long time.

Greetings from Wilshire Green

● HERBAL   ■ FRUITY   ▲ TART

This light, well-balanced spring cocktail is as pleasant to drink as it is to say. The mint and the apple brandy use the honey as a mediator to blend. Using every major bottle of bitters under the sun makes their concentrated flavors a standout taste, grounded by the earthiness of the aromatic, the aniseed of the Peychaud's, and the pithiness of the orange bitters.

The original drink this one riffs on, though its origin and exact ingredients elude me, was almost certainly called Greetings from _____ Green. As I lived in Los Angeles at the time of invention, on Wilshire Boulevard, I named it after my home.

INGREDIENTS

4 mint leaves

2 ounces (60 ml) apple brandy

2 dashes aromatic bitters

2 dashes Peychaud's bitters

2 dashes orange bitters

¾ ounce (22.5 ml) honey syrup (see page 24)

½ ounce (15 ml) lemon juice, freshly squeezed

Mint sprig, to garnish (see page 28)

METHOD

Add the mint leaves to a highball glass. Muddle gently (see page 30), being careful not to rip the mint, bringing it up the sides of the glass.

Fill the glass halfway with crushed ice.

Add the apple brandy, aromatic bitters, Peychaud's bitters, orange bitters, honey syrup, and lemon juice to a shaker.

Add ice and shake until chilled.

Strain into the prepared glass.

Top with more crushed ice and stir to combine.

Garnish with a mint sprig.

Me, Earl, and the Dancing Girl

● HERBAL　　　　　■ RICH　　　　　▲ TART

Before you get your hopes up, I've never seen the movie, nor read the book, that this cocktail's name is based on (*Me and Earl and the Dying Girl*). It's simply a clever name for a drink that calls for both Earl Grey tea and tequila. Sue me.

While formulating this drink fairly early on in my drink-making career, I tried to infuse tequila using a Christmas present I got from a friend of mine that claimed to infuse spirits with anything one's heart desires. *Claimed* is the key word there. It was very much a gimmick product designed to fool beginner mixologists. And it worked! It fooled me good.

I quickly realized that no gadgetry is needed to infuse ingredients into spirits. Just time and patience. Simply leaving one thing in another thing seems to do the trick in most cases. This drink started out as a boozy tea, but when I added an egg white, it changed the drink entirely.

INGREDIENTS

2 ounces (60 ml) Earl Grey–infused tequila (see *Method*)

¾ ounce (22.5 ml) honey syrup (see page 24)

½ ounce (15 ml) lemon juice, freshly squeezed

1 egg white

Freshly grated nutmeg, to garnish (see page 28)

METHOD

To make the Earl Grey–infused tequila: Add 1 Earl Grey tea bag per every 4 ounces tequila to a jar.

Cover and let infuse for at least 2 hours before use.

To make the cocktail: Add the infused tequila, honey syrup, lemon juice, and egg white to a shaker.

Dry shake until emulsified and frothy, about 15 seconds.

Add ice and shake until chilled.

Double strain into a chilled coupe glass. Let the froth settle for 1 to 2 minutes.

Garnish with freshly grated nutmeg.

Arnold's Plastered

● HERBAL   ■ TART   ▲ FIZZY

I'd been wanting to dive in to creating an alcoholic version of the classic Arnold Palmer for years. When the time came for me to perform that task, the decision to use interesting techniques to create a fairly basic drink seemed like the most fitting option.

The Arnold Palmer is a "mocktail" of sorts that combines unsweetened iced tea with lemonade (the American version made with water, sugar, and lemon juice). The Arnold Palmer was created by and later named after the famed golfer, whose name you can probably deduce.

When experimenting with boozy riffs on the drink, I'd recently come into possession of a lemon-flavored vodka, an extremely tart spirit that drinks more like an undersweetened liqueur. Infusing it further with English Breakfast tea mellowed it slightly. I added orange bitters and simple syrup and dragged it back from the world of fake citrus with fresh lemon juice. It's then topped off with soda water to further soften it and pay homage to what the rest of the world calls lemonade.

INGREDIENTS

2 ounces (60 ml) English Breakfast tea–infused lemon vodka (see *Method*)

2 dashes orange bitters

½ ounce (15 ml) lemon juice, freshly squeezed

¼ ounce (7.5 ml) simple syrup (see page 23)

3 ounces (90 ml) soda water

Lemon wheel, to garnish (see page 27)

METHOD

To make the tea-infused lemon vodka: Add 1 tea bag of choice (I used English Breakfast) per every 4 ounces lemon vodka (I used New Amsterdam) to a jar.

Cover and let infuse for at least 2 hours before use.

To make the cocktail: Add 2 ounces of the infused lemon vodka, orange bitters, lemon juice, and simple syrup to a shaker.

Add ice and shake until chilled.

Strain into an ice-filled highball glass.

Top with soda water.

Garnish with a lemon wheel.

Santa's Nightcap

● COFFEE   ■ CHOCOLATEY   ▲ HERBAL

My ideal evening is sitting beside a fireplace, drinking a complex, boozy dessert cocktail as I wind down with close friends, maybe a board game or two. When Christmas 2022 rolled around, I thought of Santa. Surely he's got to want that too. Even the big guy needs a break from his one day of work a year.

This coffee-y, choc-mint sipper is what first came to mind when imagining Saint Nick kicking his feet up by the fire after a long day of doing nothing. If he gets to rest, you do too.

INGREDIENTS

1¾ ounces (52.5 ml) rye whiskey

¾ ounce (22.5 ml) coffee liqueur

¾ ounce (22.5 ml) crème de cacao

¼ ounce (7.5 ml) crème de menthe

2 dashes cocoa bitters

Maraschino cherry, to garnish (see page 28)

METHOD

Add the rye, coffee liqueur, crème de cacao, crème de menthe, and cocoa bitters to a mixing glass.

Add ice and stir until chilled and diluted, 15 to 20 seconds.

Strain into an ice-filled rocks glass.

Garnish with a maraschino cherry.

Words Fail

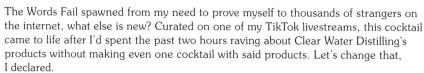

● COFFEE   ■ CHOCOLATEY   ▲ RICH

The Words Fail spawned from my need to prove myself to thousands of strangers on the internet, what else is new? Curated on one of my TikTok livestreams, this cocktail came to life after I'd spent the past two hours raving about Clear Water Distilling's products without making even one cocktail with said products. Let's change that, I declared.

Fully expecting to have to switch up ratios to find the best balance between the ingredients, as is the case when perfecting most recipes, I blindly added equal parts of every ingredient in this drink to a mixing glass, stirred it, served it over ice with an expressed orange swath, took a sip, and was immediately speechless.

The fusion of cinnamon (from Clear Water's powerful ScandaLust Cinnamon Whiskey, made by simply infusing whiskey with cinnamon); coffee (from Mr Black's, again, simple method of blending Australian vodka with specialty coffee, resulting in an assertive coffee punch); and chocolate (from the rich, velvety chocolate liqueur that is crème de cacao) makes this a stunning, sweet yet classy dessert drink that will knock the words right out of your mouth.

INGREDIENTS

**1 ounce (30 ml)
cinnamon whiskey**

**1 ounce (30 ml)
coffee liqueur**

**1 ounce (30 ml)
crème de cacao**

**Orange swath, to garnish
(see page 27)**

METHOD

Add the cinnamon whiskey, coffee liqueur, and crème de cacao to a mixing glass.

Add ice and stir until chilled and diluted, 15 to 20 seconds.

Strain into an ice-filled rocks glass.

Garnish with an expressed orange swath.

NOTE

Cinnamon "whiskeys" like Fireball often taste like cake frosting. I've used Clear Water's ScandaLust Cinnamon Whiskey for a while now. Its baking spice and raisiny notes, on top of the potent cinnamon nose and flavor, do wonders in this drink.

Affogato Martini

● COFFEE ■ CREAMY ▲ RICH

I've always had a special affinity for coffee cocktails. A good **Espresso Martini** (page 44), with a froth that rivals the densest of clouds, belongs in the cocktail hall of fame and also in my stomach, immediately.

Many people like to add an Irish cream liqueur (Baileys, usually) to their Espresso Martinis to add creaminess and simulate a richer version of a latte. While that remains more than acceptable (I'm not a huge fan of still labeling that new concoction an Espresso Martini, but I won't die on that hill), this drink calls for vanilla ice cream to be added instead, simulating an affogato.

Affogato, for those not in the know, is an Italian dessert wherein a scoop of ice cream or gelato is drowned in freshly pulled espresso. The result is a sweet, creamy nightcap that, like all desserts and dessert drinks that are worth their while, will weigh you down *and* keep you up all night. Hell yeah.

The resulting drink is frothy and creamy beyond compare and is *just* rich enough to make you want to melt into the floor while you stay up until 3 a.m. on a caffeine kick. Like the good Lord intended.

I mean, what more is there to say? Ice cream in an Espresso Martini? Shut your mouth right now and drink up.

INGREDIENTS

¾ ounce (22.5 ml) vodka

¾ ounce (22.5 ml) coffee liqueur

½ ounce (15 ml) coffee, chilled

1 tablespoon (20 g) vanilla ice cream

3 coffee beans, to garnish (see page 28)

METHOD

Add the vodka, coffee liqueur, coffee, and ice cream to a shaker.

Dry shake until emulsified and frothy, about 15 seconds.

Add ice and shake until chilled.

Double strain into a chilled coupe glass.

Garnish with 3 coffee beans.

NOTE

Using a high-quality vanilla ice cream, speckled with real vanilla, might *seem* like the way to go here. In reality, the sweetness of bulk-standard, cheap "vanilla" ice cream is key to the coffee not becoming too overpowering. Any grocery store brand should work fine.

Sundollar's Shaken Espresso

● COFFEE   ■ CREAMY   ▲ RICH

If you've opened your eyes at all since the start of the 2020s, you've likely seen posters, advertisements, and/or internet videos constantly pushing the catalyst drink for this recipe into your eyeballs. That drink, titled the Iced Brown Sugar Oat Milk Shaken Espresso (catchy), was made popular at *the café chain that shall not be named* and was latched on to by consumers everywhere, supposedly annoying the baristas, who had to shake the shots of espresso in a cocktail shaker *every time* it was ordered, to no end.

Listen, we all hate capitalism, but it turns out that sometimes it's great, because that drink is genuinely good! Making it boozy (and not getting sued in the process) proved to be a more difficult task than expected, with multiple attempts managing to somehow curdle oat milk?

Nevertheless, we pushed on, creating a drink that would feel equally at home on a bougie cocktail menu as it would in the cupholder of a 34-year-old's Nissan Versa, slowly baking in the sun as they cry in the parking lot of the job they hate. Yummy!

INGREDIENTS

1 ounce (30 ml) coffee liqueur

½ ounce (15 ml) cinnamon whiskey

2 ounces (60 ml) espresso, chilled

½ ounce (15 ml) cinnamon syrup (see page 24)

4 ounces (120 ml) milk

Freshly grated cinnamon, to garnish (see page 28)

METHOD

Add the coffee liqueur, cinnamon whiskey, espresso, and cinnamon syrup to a shaker.

Add ice and shake until chilled.

Strain into an ice-filled highball glass.

Froth milk and add to glass.

Garnish with freshly grated cinnamon.

NOTES

♦ Refrain from using oversweet cinnamon whiskey like Fireball here. Strive for a high-quality bottle, like Clear Water Distilling's ScandaLust.

♦ This is probably the only coffee cocktail where espresso is more desirable than regular brewed coffee or cold brew. In a pinch, those can be used, but it's not advised.

♦ It's not necessary, but you may sub out the regular sugar in the cinnamon syrup for brown sugar, to be more true to the original.

♦ You don't have to use oat milk like in the original drink. Any milk or plant-based alternative works great here.

Café Rouge

● COFFEE   ▨ FRUITY   ▲ RICH

This concoction was born from my need to use up the remainder of an open bottle of red wine sitting in my wine rack.

Cocktails that are made and then floated with another spirit/liquid are some of my favorite cocktails in existence. Using the fact that chocolate pairs phenomenally with both coffee and red wine separately as the basis for my argument that the latter two should also work well together (yet seeing zero internet research to back me up), I set off with my livestream audience to create the Café Rouge.

The coffee liqueur, rye whiskey, and cocoa bitters come together to make an earthy, spiced base for the sweet, fruity red wine to sit on. The more sips you take, the less of the wine remains, so the drink evolves as it's consumed. It's a phenomenal after-dinner cocktail that I'm well and truly obsessed with.

INGREDIENTS

1½ ounces (45 ml) coffee liqueur

1 ounce (30 ml) rye whiskey

2 dashes cocoa bitters

½ ounce (15 ml) demerara syrup (see page 23)

¾ ounce (22.5 ml) red wine

METHOD

Add the coffee liqueur, rye, cocoa bitters, and demerara syrup to a mixing glass.

Add ice and stir until chilled and diluted, 15 to 20 seconds.

Strain into an ice-filled rocks glass.

Float with red wine (see page 31).

NOTE

When floating a drink with red wine, it's important to use a wine you would enjoy drinking on its own, while still complementing the beverage as a whole. Most red wines work fairly well in this drink, though I'd lean toward a sweeter, fruitier one to offset the earthy coffee cocktail. I used an Australian Cabernet Sauvignon when crafting this spec. If unsure, ask your local wine store clerk—they should be more than happy to assist you. Tell 'em Nic sent you.

Funky Russian
OR WHITE RUMSHIAN

● COFFEE   ■ FUNKY   ▲ CREAMY

I was stoked when Mr Black Coffee Liqueur approached me to partner on a TikTok video, as I'd loved the brand for years. I'd never worked with a company on a brand deal before, so I had to learn the ropes quickly. The video we agreed to create together was one showcasing two different versions of a White Russian. The first was Mr Black's very simple 2:1, coffee liqueur to milk, spec. While that drink has its merits, this funkier rum-based concoction I served alongside it took the cake for me.

If I can shoehorn rum into any cocktail, I'll do it. I crafted this drink with a Jamaican Pot Still Black Rum from Hamilton, one of my favorite rums. It's specifically asked for a few times in this book (see **Hamilton Special** on page 156 and **Dad's Tea** on page 173). It's *super* funky—with a flavor that dominates (in a good way)—and this is no exception, resulting in a very, VERY funky coffee milkshake. That doesn't sound half bad, does it?

Where Mr Black decides to reach for milk in their recipe, I use half-and-half in my White Russians and variations. It's thicker and more decadent than milk but not as cloying as heavy cream. Its addition makes this recipe one of my favorite dessert drinks.

INGREDIENTS

1¾ ounces (52.5 ml) coffee liqueur

1 ounce (30 ml) funky rum (see *Notes*)

¼ ounce (7.5 ml) demerara syrup (see page 23)

1 ounce (30 ml) half-and-half

METHOD

Add the coffee liqueur, rum, and demerara syrup to an ice-filled rocks glass.

Stir until chilled.

Top with half-and-half.

Stir until incorporated, if desired.

NOTES

• Shoot for one of the funkiest aged Caribbean rums you can find here (Hamilton Jamaican Pot Still Black and Angostura 1919 are personal standouts).

• The Dude (*The Big Lebowski*) abides by half-and-half in his White Russians. I also prefer it over a heavier cream or a lighter milk, as it's a nice not-too-thick/not-too-thin middle ground. A plant-based alternative is acceptable if your stomach hates you.

Nectar of the Sods

● COFFEE   ▦ FUNKY   ▲ NUTTY

I love a layered drink, especially if the first layer provides a different texture to the second. In this nutty riff on Sasha Petraske's Dominicana, one's lips sink into a layer of luxurious yet fairly tasteless cream before breaking through to receive a funky almond coffee mixture that is sure to make even the proudest weep.

There's not much more to say here. This is the perfect blend between aperitif and full-blown dessert. Put it in your mouth.

INGREDIENTS

1½ ounces (45 ml) funky rum (see Notes)

¾ ounce (22.5 ml) coffee liqueur

¾ ounce (22.5 ml) amaretto liqueur

1 ounce (30 ml) heavy cream

3 coffee beans, to garnish (see page 28)

METHOD

Add the rum, coffee liqueur, and amaretto liqueur to a mixing glass.

Add ice and stir until chilled and diluted, 15 to 20 seconds.

Strain into a chilled coupe glass.

Float with heavy cream (see page 31).

Garnish with 3 coffee beans.

NOTES

- Shoot for one of the funkiest aged Caribbean rums you can find here (Hamilton Jamaican Pot Still Black and Angostura 1919 are personal standouts).
- Amaretto liqueur finds itself in what I call a "Listerine" situation. One brand of amaretto is so prevalent it feels like no other brand is making one, even though many probably are. I've used Disaronno since the start, it's the standard, and it's perfectly fine.
- Heavy cream is called for in this drink, as its density helps it float on top of the cocktail. Half-and-half or a plant-based alternative may work but might require some slight whipping.

◀ Top: Banane Noire; bottom: Nectar of the Sods

Banane Noire

● COFFEE   ■ NUTTY   ▲ FRUITY

This stunner of a dessert cocktail is one of the most exceptional and unique drinks I've ever tasted, and it's all thanks to Seattle-based bartender Jonathan Stanyard of @thebittergringo, one of my favorite Instagram mixology accounts, who created its catalyst, the French Espresso Martini.

The deep, rich dried fruit flavor of brandy pairs with coffee in a gorgeous, luxurious way. Pair that relationship with cocoa bitters and the sweet almond notes of orgeat, all topped off with the velvety froth of an egg white, and you've got an incredibly decadent, smooth cocktail. All that was missing, for me, was some fruitiness. The crème de banane adds a layer of punchy banana that takes this drink up a step.

If you're looking to feel like you're sitting on a cloud above the South of France, peering down at the baguettes and nude beaches below, give this one a go.

INGREDIENTS

1½ ounces (45 ml) brandy

½ ounce (15 ml) coffee liqueur

½ ounce (15 ml) crème de banane

3 dashes cocoa bitters

½ ounce (15 ml) coffee, chilled

½ ounce (15 ml) orgeat (see page 24)

1 egg white

3 coffee beans, to garnish (see page 28)

METHOD

Add the brandy, coffee liqueur, crème de banane, cocoa bitters, coffee, orgeat, and egg white to a shaker.

Dry shake until emulsified and frothy, about 15 seconds.

Add ice and shake until chilled.

Double strain into a chilled coupe glass. Let the froth settle for 1 to 2 minutes.

Garnish with 3 coffee beans.

Crepusculo

● COFFEE   ■ FUNKY   ▲ TART

Crepusculo means "twilight" in Spanish. Rather than a cocktail based around the vampirical franchise, this one evokes the feeling of the transition between day and night. Coffee meets a Margarita, bolstered by sweet vermouth, a liquid I associate with a chill, easy evening time.

In late 2021, dressed to the nines in a pinstripe suit, preparing to attend the Broadway premiere of *Mrs. Doubtfire* (a phenomenal musical, by the way) with Gabe Escobar, the social media influencer credited with creating **Gabe's Blueberry Cosmopolitan** (page 100), I felt a thirst. A thirst only quenchable by a delectable beverage. I *was* dressed up all fancy-like, so filming a video of me mixing such a beverage and subsequently posting it on TikTok only made sense to my youthful, internet-focused mind. I picked the Margarita Negra, the drink this cocktail is based on. That video went on to do surprisingly good numbers, thus beginning my true foray into social media mixology. I've yet to look back.

Pairing coffee with savory tequila doesn't sound like an obvious option, but when balanced correctly (here in equal parts), the two can complement each other perfectly. Add fruity vermouth, tart citrus, and sweetener in the form of demerara syrup (instead of the originally called-for agave), and you've got the bones of a New York Sour that's been playing tonsil tennis with a cup of coffee. And that's hot.

INGREDIENTS

1 ounce (30 ml) tequila

1 ounce (30 ml) coffee liqueur

½ ounce (15 ml) sweet vermouth

¾ ounce (22.5 ml) lime juice, freshly squeezed

¼ ounce (7.5 ml) demerara syrup (see page 23)

Lime wheel, to garnish (see page 27)

METHOD

Add the tequila, coffee liqueur, sweet vermouth, lime juice, and demerara syrup to a shaker.

Add ice and shake until chilled.

Double strain into an ice-filled rocks glass, half-rimmed with salt (see page 28).

Garnish with a lime wheel.

Post-Nut Clarity
OR ESPRESSEPINEPHRINE
OR ETHAN'S EPINEPHRINE

● COFFEE   ▣ NUTTY   ▲ RICH

Another TikTok livestream recipe, this drink was created after the viewers and I set out to create something reminiscent of a Peanut Butter Espresso Martini. While the idea sounds positively banging, getting the balance of peanut butter to coffee right turned out to be trickier than I first imagined.

A few attempts later, the drink had ended up in a rocks glass, with a square of dark chocolate on top. It was far enough away from an Espresso Martini that I felt it needed a new name. The idea of naming the drink after the infamous Peanut Butter Baby meme of the early 2000s was played with significantly, as was naming it *EpiPen* or *Epinephrine* as a reference to the caffeine in the drink energizing you much like adrenaline would to someone having an anaphylactic reaction.

While the final versions of these names have an honorable mention in the subtitle above (Espresspinephrine combining *espresso* and *epinephrine*, and Ethan's Epinephrine comedically inferring that the Peanut Butter Baby, whose name is Ethan, has a peanut allergy himself), one title was thrown at me in the final moments of my decision: Post-Nut Clarity. It's just a brilliant name on multiple levels. Coffee makes one's head clear and focused; then include the peanuts to form an innuendo—chef's kiss, truly.

By the way, if you don't know what post-nut clarity means, I really don't want to be the one to reveal that to you. Google it.

INGREDIENTS

1½ ounces (45 ml) Skrewball peanut butter whiskey

¾ ounce (22.5 ml) coffee liqueur

1 ounce (30 ml) coffee, chilled

¼ ounce (7.5 ml) simple syrup (see page 23)

1 teaspoon peanut butter

Flaky sea salt, to garnish

Peanut M&M's, to garnish

METHOD

Add the peanut butter whiskey, coffee liqueur, coffee, simple syrup, and peanut butter to a shaker.

Dry shake until emulsified, 15 seconds.

Add ice and shake until chilled.

Double strain into an ice-filled rocks glass, half-rimmed with flaky salt (see page 28).

Serve alongside a small bowl of Peanut M&M's (trust me).

NOTE

While the quality of the peanut butter doesn't play a huge part here, you may find that a more organic peanut butter lessens the sweetness of the drink. I've always used a bulk-standard grocery store brand, and I likely always will. However, do ensure the peanut butter is smooth, not chunky.

Resurrection

● BITTER   ■ CHOCOLATEY   ▲ COFFEE

The aperitif is one of my favorite kinds of cocktails: sippers one could wind down with, slowly consuming by a fire in an intimate speakeasy. This riff on Riccardo Aletta's Pura Vida is just that, and it's banging.

Capable of resurrecting the sleepiest imbiber, this rich tipple uses coffee and chocolate to lure the drinker in before hitting them with savory tequila and bitter amaro to not only wake them up but also to make them dance.

INGREDIENTS

1½ ounces (45 ml) tequila

1 ounce (30 ml)
   Averna amaro

½ ounce (15 ml)
   coffee liqueur

½ ounce (15 ml)
   crème de cacao

Orange swath, to garnish
   (see page 27)

METHOD

Add the tequila, Averna amaro, coffee liqueur, and crème de cacao to a mixing glass.

Add ice and stir until chilled and diluted, 15 to 20 seconds.

Strain into a chilled coupe glass.

Garnish with an expressed orange swath.

Bitters Sweet Symphony

● BITTER   ■ CHOCOLATEY   ▲ FRUITY

One day, somewhere in the annals of social media, I received a request to make a cocktail that could be titled Bitters Sweet Symphony, and I thought that was clever, so I did it. The result is one of the most complex drinks in this entire book.

Cramming together a heavy pour of aromatic bitters with a bunch of complementary liqueurs, a skosh of lemon juice, and a proofy bourbon proved astonishing. A wise man once said, "A drink isn't perfect when there's nothing left to add. It's perfect when there's nothing left to take away." This drink chooses not to listen to him.

Do be aware, this one's a boozer. Drink responsibly.

INGREDIENTS

1 ounce (30 ml) overproof bourbon

¾ ounce (22.5 ml) aromatic bitters

½ ounce (15 ml) crème de cacao

½ ounce (15 ml) orange liqueur

¼ ounce (7.5 ml) amaretto liqueur

2 dashes cocoa bitters

½ ounce (15 ml) lemon juice, freshly squeezed

Lemon swath, to garnish (see page 27)

METHOD

Add the overproof bourbon, aromatic bitters, crème de cacao, orange liqueur, amaretto liqueur, cocoa bitters, and lemon juice to a shaker.

Add ice and shake until chilled and diluted, 15 to 20 seconds.

Double strain into an ice-filled rocks glass.

Garnish with an expressed lemon swath.

NOTES

• The term *overproof* in any such spirit means that it has a higher alcohol content than the standard. Most bourbon brands stock an overproof; my preferred are Knob Creek and Wild Turkey, but most of them taste fairly similar in cocktails.

• You're doing a heavy pour of aromatic bitters here, so use the best. Angostura is the standard used around the world.

• Disaronno amaretto liqueur is the standard and is a completely appropriate bottle to use here. If there is an amaretto you prefer, feel free to sub it in.

Trips Abroad

● BITTER　　　■ COFFEE　　　▲ FRUITY

A boozier, more accessible riff on Nandini Khaund's Roman Holiday, this complex guzzler is an absolute stunner.

    If you love tropical cocktails, you may already be aware of a delicious drink called the Jungle Bird, which adds Campari to a fairly traditional island cocktail spec. The Roman Holiday (and in turn Trips Abroad) is the Olympic gymnast to the Jungle Bird's four-year-old on a trampoline. Wildly complex and mind-boggling to the taste buds, this drink has the possibility of shocking even the most accomplished drinker.

INGREDIENTS

1 ounce (30 ml) Averna amaro

½ ounce (15 ml) Aperol

1 ounce (30 ml) coffee liqueur

¾ ounce (22.5 ml) orange juice

¾ ounce (22.5 ml) lime juice, freshly squeezed

¼ ounce (7.5 ml) demerara syrup (see page 23)

Small pinch of salt

Cinnamon stick, to garnish (optional)

METHOD

Fill a double rocks glass halfway with crushed ice.

Add the Averna amaro, Aperol, coffee liqueur, orange juice, lime juice, demerara syrup, and pinch of salt to a shaker.

Add ice and shake until chilled.

Strain into prepared glass and top with more crushed ice.

Garnish with an optional cinnamon stick.

NOTES

- Essentially sweetened Campari, Aperol may be subbed out for Campari here for a slightly drier, more bitter drink. Just add a skosh more demerara syrup.

- Be sure to use freshly squeezed or 100 percent real orange juice here, not from concentrate, or you risk an unbalanced cocktail.

- While we're talking about the tiniest pinch of salt here, don't skip it. The minute amount elevates this cocktail to new heights.

Mezcal Dalnegroni

● BITTER　　■ COFFEE　　▲ SMOKY

Hey, remember Dalgona coffee? The trend that took over the internet at the beginning of 2020 that led millions of lonely quarantiners to whip air into instant coffee and be excited by that? Simpler times.

A year or so post-pandemic, I saw a cocktail menu item at a bar in New York that had Dalgona in its title. Intrigued, I swore to one day create a concoction of my own that incorporated the whipped coffee. I was able to realize this idea some time later by merging mezcal, a **Negroni** (page 53), and Dalgona coffee into a beverage I am, to this day, consistently and wildly excited by.

The bitter notes of instant coffee and Campari, the sweetness of the sugar in the Dalgona, and the sweet vermouth combine with the smoky mezcal to create an insanely complex beverage that is well worth the time and effort it calls for.

INGREDIENTS

½ ounce (15 ml) boiling water

1 tablespoon instant coffee

1 tablespoon sugar

1 ounce (30 ml) mezcal

1 ounce (30 ml) Campari

1 ounce (30 ml) sweet vermouth

3 coffee beans, to garnish (see page 28)

METHOD

To make the Dalgona whipped coffee: Add the boiling water, instant coffee, and sugar to a mixing bowl.

Whip until thick and frothy, set aside.

To make the cocktail: Add the mezcal, Campari, and sweet vermouth to a separate mixing glass.

Add ice and stir until chilled and diluted.

Strain into an ice-filled double rocks glass.

Top with the Dalgona whipped coffee.

Garnish with 3 coffee beans.

NOTE

Dalgona coffee is traditionally made using instant coffee. In every other scenario, I'd ask you to steer away from the ingredient, but it is fairly necessary here to achieve the foam you're striving for. Aim for a fairly high-quality brand if you feel it's imperative.

Nudey Rudy

● BITTER ▓ FRUITY ▲ HERBAL

If you weren't already aware of my passion for drink-making, one glance at my Instagram Explore page would quickly key you in. My scrolling is lined with cocktail creations of all sorts, some of which intrigue me so much that I save them to test later. One of these was the catalyst for this cocktail.

Marcus Brito's (@shakestrain) Naked and Falling in Love, a riff on the Naked and Famous, which in itself is a riff on the Last Word, is a delightful cocktail that dulls the citric nature of the latter two cocktails by splitting the original lime juice with fresh orange juice. My Nudey Rudy takes that idea one step further and replaces the mezcal in Falling in Love with tequila and the Campari with its sweeter cousin, Aperol, to calm the whole drink down a little bit, making it a delightfully chill sipper.

INGREDIENTS

1 ounce (30 ml) tequila

1 ounce (30 ml) Aperol

1 ounce (30 ml) Benedictine

½ ounce (15 ml) orange juice

¼ ounce (7.5 ml) lime juice, freshly squeezed

Orange swath, to garnish (see page 27)

METHOD

Add the tequila, Aperol, Benedictine, orange juice, and lime juice to a shaker.

Add ice and shake until chilled.

Double strain into an ice-filled rocks glass.

Garnish with an expressed orange swath.

NOTES

◆ Essentially sweetened Campari, Aperol may be subbed out for Campari here for a slightly drier, more bitter drink. There are no perfect substitutes.

◆ Be sure to use freshly squeezed or 100 percent real orange juice here, not from concentrate, or you risk an unbalanced cocktail.

Debbie Did It

● BITTER   ▦ FRUITY   ▲ TART

This creation is the first drink I remember making to impress a group of friends.

Drinking with good people, listening to music, and playing some sort of board game or outdoor activity is one of my favorite pasttimes. Doing so genuinely makes me very close to the happiest I can get. Add in sharing my very own cocktail recipes with those people and, well, I might just weep.

After curating Debbie Did It, my riff on Zachary Gelnaw-Rubin's Debbie, Don't, I brought a few jars of it to a friend's place. When I arrived, I added ice to the jars and shook it like you would a shaker. Straining into a separate glass was optional, but leaving it in the jar and consuming it from there turned into a fairly common practice throughout the evening. This started a tradition of me jarring a few different drinks and having my buddies be unknowing guinea pigs for my early recipes as we played cornhole or some version of a card game.

Debbie, Don't is already such a stunning drink. Tequila and maple bounce off the lime, not unlike a maple Margarita. This variation adds a touch more bitterness and flavor by way of Campari and orange liqueur to make all the Negroni fans out there happy.

INGREDIENTS

1¼ ounces (37.5 ml) tequila

¾ ounce (22.5 ml) Campari

½ ounce (15 ml) orange liqueur

¾ ounce (22.5 ml) lime juice, freshly squeezed

½ ounce (15 ml) maple syrup

Lime wheel, to garnish (see page 27)

METHOD

Add the tequila, Campari, orange liqueur, lime juice, and maple syrup to a shaker.

Add ice and shake until chilled.

Double strain into a chilled coupe glass.

Garnish with a lime wheel.

Haich Tee

● BITTER   ▦ FRUITY   ▲ NUTTY

Cocktails that use a heavy pour of bitters rather than the usual dash or two can be some of the most exciting. I love this style of drink, as seen in **Bitters Sweet Symphony** (page 139) and **Jaffa Kick** (page 66). The concentrated flavor (no, they aren't any more alcoholic than most liquors) can introduce a drinker to a completely new taste profile while not being too difficult to acquire.

Named after Haiti, the country where the creator of Peychaud's bitters was born, and how people from my country say the letter *h*, Haich Tee is a riff on the aromatic bitters–heavy Trinidad Sour, perhaps the defining drink of that category.

Peychaud's bitters are licorice-y and bright red, so a heavy pour backed up by equally powerful ingredients results in a cocktail that is both fun and complex.

INGREDIENTS

1 ounce (30 ml) Peychaud's bitters

¾ ounce (22.5 ml) gin

¾ ounce (22.5 ml) lime juice, freshly squeezed

½ ounce (15 ml) orgeat (see page 24)

½ ounce (15 ml) raspberry syrup (see page 24)

Lemon swath, to garnish (see page 27)

Raspberries, to garnish (optional)

METHOD

Add the Peychaud's bitters, gin, lime juice, orgeat, and raspberry syrup to a shaker.

Add ice and shake until chilled.

Double strain into a chilled coupe glass.

Garnish with an expressed lemon swath and an optional cocktail pick of raspberries.

NOTE

Peychaud's is the brand name of an anise-flavored (licorice-y) bitters. You're doing a heavy pour of Peychaud's here, so use the proper stuff.

Tequila Me Elmo

● BITTER   ▓ HERBAL   ▲ FRUITY

It's time to celebrate Elmo, the bright red Muppet we all know and love. The name was thought up as a part of my Cocktail Name Game on a livestream, and I ran with it.

The "requirements" (rules I made up to make life harder for myself) were: It had to be red, served neat/up (not on the rocks, as Elmo doesn't like fellow Muppet Zoe's rock friend Rocco), and complex (because I wouldn't strive for anything less). So was born Tequila Me Elmo.

Almost a very distant riff on a **Sazerac** (page 58), the bitter Campari and savory tequila work surprisingly well with the sweet raspberry syrup, the aniseed-y absinthe, and the bitter Peychaud's to create a flavor bomb that rivals anything Rocco could even dream of making in his lifetime.

Maybe one day I'll be invited to the speakeasy on Sesame Street and get all the puppets absolutely sloshed.

One day.

INGREDIENTS

Absinthe, to rinse (see *Note*)

1½ ounces (45 ml) tequila

¾ ounce (22.5 ml) Campari

2 dashes Peychaud's bitters

½ ounce (15 ml) raspberry syrup (see page 24)

Lemon swath, to garnish (see page 27)

METHOD

Rinse a chilled snifter or Gibraltar glass with absinthe (see page 27).

Add the tequila, Campari, Peychaud's bitters, and raspberry syrup to a mixing glass.

Add ice to the mixing glass and stir until chilled and diluted, 15 to 20 seconds.

Strain into the prepared glass.

Garnish with an expressed lemon swath.

NOTE

You'd be hard-pressed to find an absinthe that doesn't taste like most other absinthes on the market. Get a bottle that looks pretty, for it's rare that a recipe will call for more than a dash or a rinsing. It'll be on your bar for years to come.

Cupid's Chokehold

● BITTER   ▥ SMOKY   ▲ SPICY

Cupid's Chokehold, much like the **Lonely Valentine** (page 65), is a cocktail that doesn't taste how it appears. Sweet and pink, with a sugared rim adding to the look of innocence, its flavor is actually that of fiery ginger, bitter Campari, and smoky, peaty Scotch whisky. This, to me, mirrors the feeling of being alone on Valentine's Day. While one may pretend not to care about the holiday, inside they likely feel bitter and volatile.

Hatred of societal expectations aside, this is an absolutely delicious cocktail. A variation on the **Penicillin** (page 56), this one adds Campari to the mix, which works perfectly to counter the sweetness and smokiness of the drink with its bitter notes.

INGREDIENTS

1 ounce (30 ml) blended Scotch whisky

1 ounce (30 ml) Campari

1 ounce (30 ml) ginger syrup (see page 25)

½ ounce (15 ml) lemon juice, freshly squeezed

½ ounce (15 ml) Islay Scotch whisky

Candied ginger, to garnish (see page 27)

Lemon swath, to garnish (see page 27)

METHOD

Add the blended Scotch, Campari, ginger syrup, and lemon juice to a shaker.

Add ice and shake until chilled.

Double strain into an ice-filled rocks glass, half-rimmed with sugar (see page 28).

Float with Islay Scotch (see page 31).

Garnish with candied ginger or an expressed lemon swath.

Bin Chicken

● FUNKY   ■ BITTER   ▲ FRUITY

A riff on the classic Jungle Bird, already one of my faves, this drink's nutty, bitter complexity makes me feel like I'm flying, unlike its namesake.

The white ibis, a feral creature that roams the streets and beaches of my home country, stealing people's picnic food and digging through trash cans before scampering off to annoy a tourist, is an Australian icon. Its nickname, the Bin Chicken, has worked its way into the Australian lexicon, so much so that I regularly forget its real name.

While others may claim the emu or cockatoo is the national bird of Australia, this dastardly beast, while putrid and foul, gets my vote. It represents who we are as a people. We're gross; we're kind of stupid; we have long, gangly legs . . . maybe I'm just thinking of my brother. Regardless, make this drink, guzzle it by the nearest BBQ, and sing our national anthem. I'll start.

"Waltzing Matilda . . . "

INGREDIENTS

1 ounce (30 ml) funky rum (see *Notes*)

1 ounce (30 ml) whiskey (see *Notes*)

¾ ounce (22.5 ml) Campari

2 dashes aromatic bitters

1½ ounces (45 ml) pineapple juice

¾ ounce (22.5 ml) lime juice, freshly squeezed

¾ ounce (22.5 ml) orgeat (see page 24)

Small pinch of salt

Pineapple fronds, to garnish (see page 28)

Lime wheel, to garnish (see page 27)

METHOD

Add the rum, whiskey, Campari, aromatic bitters, pineapple juice, lime juice, orgeat, and salt to a shaker.

Add ice and shake until chilled.

Double strain into an ice-filled rocks glass.

Garnish with pineapple fronds and a lime wheel.

NOTES

- Shoot for one of the funkiest aged Caribbean rums you can find here (Hamilton Jamaican Pot Still Black and Angostura 1919 are personal standouts).

- Australian whiskey is optional here, but you would get brownie points if you procured one. Bourbon or rye would both work just fine.

- While we're talking about the tiniest pinch of salt here, don't skip it. The minute amount elevates this cocktail to new heights.

Mule Ride

● FUNKY   ■ FIZZY   ▲ SPICY

The **Moscow Mule** (page 52), along with similar (tame, simple) drinks, such as the **Whiskey Sour** (page 60), were the first cocktails I would consume on the regular when I moved to LA, and they are the answers I give when anyone asks me what drinks to start with when getting into mixology. So it's only fitting that, as far as I can remember, this drink was the result of one of my first forays into creating my own cocktails.

The seemingly simple substitute of vodka for rye elevates this Mule to something that tastes like more than just tart ginger beer. If a high-quality, full-bodied whiskey is used, its flavor shines through the ginger beer much like it does in a good whiskey–ginger ale, my preferred dive bar order.

INGREDIENTS

2 ounces (60 ml) rye whiskey

¾ ounce (22.5 ml) lime juice

¼ ounce (7.5 ml) demerara syrup (see page 23)

6 ounces (180 ml) ginger beer

Lime wedge, to garnish (see page 27)

METHOD

Add the rye, lime juice, and demerara syrup to an ice-filled highball glass or copper mug. Stir to combine.

Top with ginger beer.

Garnish with a lime wedge.

NOTES

- Bundaberg ginger beer is my nostalgic choice; however, more fiery brands like Cock 'n Bull and Goslings are also suitable.

- To make a Mule Ride in the Orchard, sub out the demerara syrup and 3 ounces of ginger beer with 2½ ounces (75 ml) hard apple cider to give the drink a unique punch.

Sweet Rum Rickey

A Rickey is any cocktail that contains a spirit and a citrus, topped with seltzer. Named in the 1880s after "Colonel Joe" Rickey, who preferred his Whiskey Highballs with a skosh of lime juice, the Rickey is the perfect beverage for when it's hot enough outside to fry an egg on the hood of one's 2001 Mitsubishi Lancer station wagon (RIP my first car, Lancerlot).

My preferred summer Rickey cocktail is this Sweet Rum Rickey. Its simple flavors allow the funkiness of the rum to really shine if one were to go with an aged Caribbean bottle, but even a tamer light rum would be acceptable here to lean the cocktail into the realm of the more airy, more popular Gin Rickey.

The Rickey is a drink that isn't generally given too much thought when one discusses or teaches drinkers about classic cocktails, but it absolutely should be. A well-made Rickey is one of the best options in the category of summer pool party drinks. They're easy to make and will easily please a whole horde of drunk, wet partygoers with little to no effort.

INGREDIENTS

1½ ounces (45 ml) rum

¾ ounce (22.5 ml) lime juice, freshly squeezed

½ ounce (15 ml) simple syrup (see page 23)

3½ ounces (105 ml) soda water

Lime wedge, to garnish (see page 27)

METHOD

Add the rum, lime juice, and simple syrup to a shaker.

Add ice and shake until chilled.

Strain into an ice-filled highball glass.

Top with soda water.

Garnish with a lime wedge.

NOTES

♦ Any rum would work in this drink. I personally like using the punchiest Jamaican rums in cocktails where the rum is the overriding flavor, but white rum or a tamer demerara rum would both fit fine here.

♦ If you're in a rush, this one can be built in the glass instead of shaken. The resulting drink will be less diluted and harsher, so take off ¼ ounce of the lime juice.

Hamilton Special

● FUNKY　　　　■ FRUITY　　　　▲ BITTER

I often find myself in situations wherein I'm searching for a name to attach to a cocktail I've just created. It's not uncommon for this to happen in front of people. When it does, one suggestion always arises:

"Name it after yourself! Call it The Nic or something."

Setting aside that terrible (yet far too frequent) example, my answer is always the same: "No, no, no. I'll know when a drink fully encapsulates my vibe and personality. For now, let's just call this one **Post-Nut Clarity**" (page 137).

Nearing the midpoint of 2022, I found myself becoming bored of this same refrain. Not only did it feel pretentious to suggest my name deserves the perfect drink, but monotony is famously not in my brain's wheelhouse. So, going against my own idea that the perfect drink to attach my name to would happen across me one day, I set out to put that frequent conversation to bed.

It was simpler than I'd imagined it would be. Turns out I'm no more complex than putting all my favorite flavors in a glass over ice. The result of my endeavors was this (in theory) Rum Port Reverse Manhattan Negroni that I labeled the Hamilton Special. Because it just *is*.

INGREDIENTS

1¾ ounces (52.5 ml) tawny port

1 ounce (30 ml) Hamilton Jamaican Pot Still Black Rum

¼ ounce (7.5 ml) Campari

2 dashes aromatic bitters

1 dash orange bitters

Lemon swath, to garnish (see page 27)

Maraschino cherry, to garnish (see page 28)

METHOD

Add the tawny port, rum, Campari, aromatic bitters, and orange bitters to a mixing glass.

Add ice and stir until chilled and diluted, 15 to 20 seconds.

Strain into a chilled coupe glass.

Garnish with an expressed lemon swath and a maraschino cherry.

NOTES

◆ Port is a fortified wine that must originate in Portugal. It is funky when well aged, and funk lends itself to this cocktail phenomenally. When formulating this recipe, I used W&J Graham's 20 Year Tawny Port, but any similarly aged tawny should work here. Oloroso or Amontillado sherry may be used as a substitute.

◆ Jamaican rums are some of the funkiest, most flavorful spirits on the market. My personal favorite is Hamilton's Jamaican Pot Still Black Rum, not only because the brand and I share a name but because Hamilton's line of rums is positively finger-licking. Any good-quality, funky Caribbean rum should work as a substitute.

French Bogan

● FUNKY   ▓ FRUITY   ▲ TART

Much like the **Bramble** (page 40), this is less a layered drink and more a marbled one. The banana funk of the rum and the mature fruitiness of the brandy blend perfectly with a heavy pour of pineapple juice. The mixture is then poured over a layer of grenadine (feel free to use any berry syrup) to create the look of a Frenchman's sunburn while visiting the Australian outback.

The Hawaiian Redneck, the cocktail that the French Bogan riffs upon, uses sweeter Southern Comfort in place of the brandy and tamer white rum in place of the funky stuff. This riff is more adult and complex while maintaining the original's playful roots.

INGREDIENTS

1 ounce (30 ml) brandy

1 ounce (30 ml) funky rum (see Note)

3 ounces (90 ml) pineapple juice

¼ ounce (7.5 ml) grenadine (see page 23)

Pineapple fronds, to garnish (see page 28)

METHOD

Add the brandy, rum, and pineapple juice to a mixing glass.

Add ice and stir until chilled and diluted, 15 to 20 seconds.

Add grenadine to the bottom of a double rocks glass and add ice.

Strain the mixture into the double rocks glass.

Garnish with pineapple fronds and a cocktail umbrella.

NOTE

Shoot for one of the funkiest aged Caribbean rums you can find here (Hamilton Jamaican Pot Still Black and Angostura 1919 are personal standouts).

No Takesies-Backsies

● FUNKY ■ HERBAL ▲ COFFEE

A boozier riff on Barback's Revenge, which was conceived by Anders Erickson, one of my favorite online cocktail creators, No Takesies-Backsies is essentially a funky, coffee-y **Manhattan** (page 48).

If you like the sound of that, you're in the right place. If you feel it's maybe too boozy for you *and* you have all the time in the world (you unemployed sod, you), feel free to sub out the coffee liqueur for 1 ounce (30 ml) of homemade cold brew concentrate to make the original. I'm not your dad.

INGREDIENTS

1 ounce (30 ml) funky rum (see *Notes*)

1 ounce (30 ml) Benedictine

½ ounce (15 ml) coffee liqueur

½ ounce (15 ml) Amontillado sherry

Lemon swath, to garnish (see page 27)

METHOD

Add the rum, Benedictine, coffee liqueur, and Amontillado sherry to a mixing glass.

Add ice and stir until chilled and diluted, 15 to 20 seconds.

Strain into a chilled coupe glass.

Garnish with an expressed lemon swath.

NOTES

◆ Shoot for one of the funkiest aged Caribbean rums you can find here (Hamilton Jamaican Pot Still Black and Angostura 1919 are personal standouts).

◆ Sherry is, like vermouth and port, a type of fortified wine. Amontillado is funky and dark, pairing with the rum in this drink like a match made in heaven. Oloroso sherry or a good sweet vermouth may be used as substitutes here, resulting in slightly different beverages.

Drive My Sidecar

Created on a TikTok livestream in celebration of the 94th Academy Awards and the nominees within them, Drive My Sidecar is a drink made in reference to the lone international feature to be nominated for Best Picture that year, Japan's *Drive My Car.*

Replacing the brandy in a traditional Sidecar (a drink I've never really enjoyed) with the more mellow, funky sake while lowering the amount of citrus and making up the lost measure in a slightly fiery ginger syrup turns a bracing cocktail into this softer, dulcet one that celebrates the sake and perfectly balances it with the bitter, sour, and sweet notes from the other ingredients. Now that this drink exists, I'm not sure I'll drink another regular, plain-Jane Sidecar again.

INGREDIENTS

1½ ounces (45 ml) nama (unpasteurized) sake

¾ ounce (22.5 ml) orange liqueur

½ ounce (15 ml) lemon juice, freshly squeezed

¼ ounce (7.5 ml) ginger syrup (see page 25)

Lemon swath, to garnish (see page 27)

METHOD

Add the sake, orange liqueur, lemon juice, and ginger syrup to a shaker.

Add ice and shake until chilled.

Double strain into a chilled coupe glass.

Garnish with an expressed lemon swath.

NOTE

Sake's varietals are as vast as wine, and each serves a different purpose. In my research, I've found that nama (unpasteurized) sake lends itself to most mixology the best, as it has that stunning, funky sake flavor you're likely searching for without overpowering the cocktail or disappearing into the drink.

Read to Filth

● FUNKY   ■ RICH   ▲ FRUITY

One of my favorite pastimes is watching catty drag queens "read" (roast, critique) each other "to filth" (thoroughly, no holding back) on reality television. I'm sure I would cry if I was on the receiving end of any of these reads, so I'll stick to drinking this riff on Matt Tocco's Expense of Honesty.

Funky rum and the pleasant sweetness of bourbon are paired with a splash of grenadine and bolstered by two different bitters to craft a sexy, rich, funky cocktail that rivals the sexiest, richest, funkiest queens working today. I'm looking at you, Symone. ;)

INGREDIENTS

1½ ounces (45 ml) funky rum (see *Note*)

1 ounce (30 ml) bourbon

2 dashes aromatic bitters

2 dashes Peychaud's bitters

¾ ounce (22.5 ml) grenadine (see page 23)

Orange swath, to garnish (see page 27)

METHOD

Add the rum, bourbon, aromatic bitters, Peychaud's bitters, and grenadine to a mixing glass.

Add ice and stir until chilled and diluted, 15 to 20 seconds.

Strain into a chilled coupe glass.

Garnish with an expressed orange swath.

NOTE

Shoot for one of the funkiest aged Caribbean rums you can find here (Hamilton Jamaican Pot Still Black and Angostura 1919 are personal standouts).

Tub-Thumper

● FUNKY   ■ NUTTY   ▲ FIZZY

This tall guzzler is a refreshingly nutty take on the cocktail that marked my first foray into the world of proper mixology, and it's delectable.

The Añejo Highball, a riff on the classic Dark 'n' Stormy, was created by legendary drink-maker and personal mixology icon of mine, Dale DeGroff, in New York City somewhere near the turn of the 21st century as a tribute to the great Cuban bartenders of the 1900s. A good transitional drink from the **Moscow Mules** (page 52), the ginger beer–based highball also taught me just how much I love rum. I riffed on it even further here, adding amaretto liqueur in place of the original orange liqueur.

My ex and I would take these down to my apartment building's hot tub and drink them out of plastic sippy cups to comply with the "no glass in the swimming area" rule. Feel free to continue that tradition for me.

INGREDIENTS

1½ ounces (45 ml) funky rum (see *Notes*)

½ ounce (15 ml) amaretto liqueur

2 dashes aromatic bitters

½ ounce (15 ml) lime juice

6 ounces (180 ml) ginger beer

Lime wedge, to garnish (see page 27)

METHOD

Add the rum, amaretto liqueur, aromatic bitters, and lime juice to a shaker.

Add ice and shake until chilled.

Strain into an ice-filled highball glass.

Top with ginger beer.

Garnish with a lime wedge.

NOTES

- Use a funky *añejo* (aged) Caribbean rum here (Hamilton Jamaican Pot Still Black and Smith & Cross are excellent), as anything tamer will cower behind the powerful ginger beer.
- There are many amaretto liqueurs, but Disaronno is the standard. I've used it since the start.
- Bundaberg ginger beer is my nostalgic choice; however, fiery brands like Cock & Bull and Goslings are also suitable.

Axel Reese

● CREAMY   ■ CHOCOLATEY   ▲ NUTTY

Originally named My Brother Reese (an absolutely meh name), this drink was renamed in commemoration of TikTok megastar Axel Webber. Axel made a name for himself after showcasing his "tiny" NYC apartment to the world and rode that wave to stardom.

I, being the social media shill I have become, made a TikTok dedicating this drink to Axel, and it remains one of my favorite dessert cocktails I've ever created.

Made with peanut butter (Axel's favorite food, it seems) in both jarred and infused-whiskey form, cheap chocolate syrup, and a very funky rum, this intensely rich cocktail plays with the idea of being a liquid Reese's Peanut Butter Cup, and boy does it play *well*. The addition of flaky sea salt and dark chocolate as garnishes matures this drink just the right amount while the milk works as a thinning agent, making the drink feel less like pudding and more like a delicious dessert beverage.

INGREDIENTS

1½ ounces (45 ml) Skrewball peanut butter whiskey

½ ounce (15 ml) rum

1½ ounces (45 ml) chocolate syrup

½ ounce (15 ml) milk

1 tablespoon peanut butter

1 ounce (30 ml) milk

Square of dark chocolate, to garnish

Flaky sea salt, to garnish

METHOD

Add the peanut butter whiskey, rum, chocolate syrup, ½ ounce (15 ml) milk, and peanut butter to a shaker.

Add ice and shake until chilled.

Double strain into an ice-filled rocks glass.

Float with 1 ounce (30 ml) milk (see page 31).

Garnish with a square of dark chocolate and a pinch of flaky sea salt.

NOTES

- The rum used in this drink is drinker's choice, just make it dark. It works with either an extremely funky rum like Hamilton Jamaican Pot Still Black or Smith & Cross, or a tamer one like Appleton Estate Signature Blend or Hamilton Demerara.

- Feel free to splurge on an expensive chocolate syrup here. Hershey's works just fine too.

- Full-fat milk is actually less desirable here. Go for a low-fat or plant-based alternative, as the goal is to thin the cocktail out so it's not so pudding-like.

- While the quality of the peanut butter doesn't play a huge part here, a more organic peanut butter lessens the sweetness of the drink. I've always used a standard grocery store brand, and I likely always will. However, ensure the peanut butter is smooth, not chunky.

- I've never done this, but swapping out the dark chocolate garnish with a Justin's Dark Chocolate Peanut Butter Cup sounds like absolute heaven.

Different Year

● **CREAMY**　　　▨ **FRUITY**　　　▲ **BITTER**

This drink was invented to commemorate the release of my debut single, "Different Year," on January 8, 2021. Written and released at the height of the pandemic, the song tries to demonstrate the feeling of wanting to go to sleep and wake up when it's all over. It's a very sad song hidden behind a poppy, happy track, like someone trying to hide what they're truly feeling.

The merchandising motif of the song, for whatever reason, was an image of the sun coming out from behind a cloud. So, when crafting a cocktail to honor my attempted entry into the music industry, I wanted to play with that image. My immediate plan was to make it blue. Like the sky!

Blue drinks, to me, always scream tropical. Tropical drinks are famous for having a ton of ingredients and beachy flavors. I chucked some cream of coconut, lemon juice, and more bitters than is perhaps usual for a Piña Colada riff into a shaker with some blue curaçao, and out came the Different Year.

Now, legally, you have to listen to the song when you drink this drink. It's the law . . . I can't change the law. *I'd be lying if I said* I was sorry.

INGREDIENTS

1½ ounces (45 ml) white rum

¾ ounce (22.5 ml) blue curaçao

2 dashes orange bitters

1 dash Angostura bitters

½ ounce (15 ml) cream of coconut

½ ounce (15 ml) lemon juice, freshly squeezed

Lemon wheel, to garnish (see page 27)

METHOD

Add the rum, blue curaçao, orange bitters, Angostura bitters, cream of coconut, and lemon juice to a shaker.

Add ice and shake until chilled.

Double strain into a chilled coupe glass.

Garnish with a lemon wheel.

NOTE

Blue curaçao is simply orange liqueur dyed blue. It's used in a bunch of tropical drinks to make sloshed resort-goers interested in their cocktails. If you're not as easily aroused, you could sub in any orange liqueur here. Cointreau, Pierre Ferrand's Dry Curaçao, and Luxardo's Triplum Triple Sec are all great options.

Flipsy-Doozy

● CREAMY   ■ FRUITY   ▲ NUTTY

A flip is any cocktail that uses an egg yolk or a whole egg to thicken the drink and make it creamy and dreamy, and I've always been partial to one. The Café Con Leche Flip and the Gaelic Flip are two of my favorite cocktails on the planet, not to mention the humble **Eggnog** (page 43), the most famous flip of them all.

This is my contribution to the flip world: a thick, creamy, and hearty beverage that takes influence from already existing flips to carve out a space of its own. The spicy rye, sweet vermouth, and nutty orgeat create a funky balance that rivals Earth, Wind & Fire.

INGREDIENTS

1¼ ounces (37.5 ml)
   rye whiskey

1 ounce (30 ml)
   sweet vermouth

½ ounce (15 ml) orgeat
   (see page 24)

⅓ ounce (15 ml)
   heavy cream

1 egg

Freshly grated nutmeg
   or cinnamon, to
   garnish (see page 28)

METHOD

Add the rye, sweet vermouth, orgeat, heavy cream, and whole egg to a shaker.

Dry shake until emulsified, 15 seconds.

Add ice and shake until chilled.

Double strain into a chilled coupe glass.

Garnish with freshly grated nutmeg or cinnamon.

NOTES

• You can substitute a plant-based alternative for the heavy cream, but the resulting drink will be thinner. Don't use "creamer," as I'm not sure I even know what it is.

• Shaking a whole egg or yolk into a drink can give it a lovely, custard-y texture. Flips and Eggnog riffs use them regularly. As opposed to the egg white, there's not a great substitute for whole eggs or yolks in cocktails. Use them here or make something else!

Dad's Tea

● CREAMY   ▦ FUNKY   ▲ RICH

This drink was crafted in celebration of my father's 60th birthday. Baileys Irish Cream on the rocks was always the adults' treat during Hamilton family getaways, so blending that concept with my dad's preferred cup of tea spec (tea, milk, and honey) seemed like the way to go.

Tea is a massive part of Australian culture, albeit not as much as the Brits'. But it's rare you'll find an Australian parent who doesn't settle down with a cuppa every night before bed, sipping on it while watching the tele. Uniquely, we're freezing our tea here. Shaking the drink with this "tea ice" and subsequently dumping it into the glass imparts just enough tea flavor without it overwhelming the cocktail.

This recipe is one of the best dessert drinks that's come from my brain. Papa Bear should be proud.

INGREDIENTS

Brewed English Breakfast tea

1¼ ounces (37.5 ml) **Irish cream liqueur**

½ ounce (15 ml) **Hamilton Demerara Rum**

¼ ounce (7.5 ml) **Hamilton Jamaican Pot Still Black Rum**

¾ ounce (22.5 ml) **honey syrup (see page 24)**

½ ounce (15 ml) **milk**

METHOD

To make the tea ice: Pour the brewed tea into an ice cube tray and freeze. Make enough for 5 to 6 ice cubes per serving.

Leave until fully frozen.

To make the cocktail: Add the Irish cream, demerara rum, Jamaican rum, honey syrup, and milk to a shaker.

Add tea ice cubes to the shaker and vigorously shake until chilled and ice is broken up, 15 to 20 seconds.

Dump (see page 31) into a rocks glass.

NOTES

◆ I've always been partial to a peppermint tea over a brown tea, contrary to most Australians. My dad recently confessed to me that he has also been drinking more peppermint tea lately, but as we're making ice out of the tea that we use here, go for a darker varietal, such as English Breakfast or Earl Grey.

◆ Baileys is the obvious choice when it comes to Irish cream liqueurs. On the off chance that your liquor store doesn't stock it, most other Irish creams on the market taste as good if not better.

◆ This recipe is one of a minority in this book that calls for a specific brand, in this case rum. Aside from the facts that Hamilton is my preferred rum brand and it shares its name with

the surname of my father, the blend of these two specific rums is *stunning* in this cocktail. If you must substitute for them, use a blend of your favorite funky and tame rums.

◆ Full-fat milk is actually less desirable here. Go for a low-fat or plant-based alternative, as the goal is to thin the cocktail out so it's not so pudding-like.

Peanut Butter Grasshopper

● **CREAMY** ■ **NUTTY** ▲ **CHOCOLATEY**

There's a reason the Grasshopper, the minty 1919 classic, transcended Prohibition and has continued to be a mainstay on many cocktail bars around the world to this day. It's insanely yet innocently delicious. Make it peanut-buttery? You must be kidding me!

Eerily reminiscent of melted peanut butter ice cream, this extremely simple drink is a variation of a classic that has since become but a canvas for bartenders of all types to riff upon. This recipe follows the original equal-parts spec with heavy cream, but you'll often see the Grasshopper and its riffs listed as a blended drink with ice cream. Either way, it's a drink that, when my then boyfriend and I first drafted it, baffled us by how tasty it was and how easy it was to drink. You could down a true ton of Peanut Butter Grasshoppers with relative ease—if you're not allergic to lactose or nuts, of course.

INGREDIENTS

1¼ ounces (37.5 ml) Skrewball peanut butter whiskey

1¼ ounces (37.5 ml) crème de cacao

1¼ ounces (37.5 ml) heavy cream

Freshly grated dark chocolate, to garnish (see page 28)

METHOD

Add the peanut butter whiskey, crème de cacao, and heavy cream to a shaker.

Add ice and shake until chilled.

Double strain into a chilled coupe glass.

Garnish with freshly grated dark chocolate.

Amarolada

● CREAMY   ■ BITTER   ▲ FRUITY

I can't get enough of riffing on the **Piña Colada** (page 57), as evidenced by my other riffs, the **Different Year** (page 169), **Woah There Mambo** (page 99), and **Bit of Respite** (page 176)—see both the Amarolada and Bit of Respite pictured on page 177. This one draws inspiration from Zac Overman's Angostura Colada, replacing the heavy pour of aromatic bitters with an exact ratio of one of my favorite liqueur categories, the amaro.

Overproof rum is used here as an equally intense backboard for the bitter liqueur. Combining the rum and the amaro with the Colada classics (pineapple, coconut, and lime) results in a powerful yet strangely smooth drink—a truly adult alternative to the easygoing Piña.

INGREDIENTS

1½ ounces (45 ml)
  Averna amaro

½ ounce (15 ml)
  overproof rum

2 ounces (60 ml)
  pineapple juice

1½ ounces (45 ml)
  cream of coconut

1 ounce (30 ml) lime
  juice, freshly squeezed

Lime wheel, to garnish
  (see page 27)

METHOD

Add the Averna amaro, overproof rum, pineapple juice, cream of coconut, and lime juice to a shaker.

Add ice and shake until chilled.

Dump (see page 31) into a chilled wineglass or hurricane glass.

Garnish with a lime wheel and a cocktail umbrella.

NOTE

The term *overproof* in any such spirit means that it has a higher alcohol content than the standard. My go-to overproof rum is Wray & Nephew.

Bit of Respite

● CREAMY   ■ CHOCOLATEY   ▲ HERBAL

A riff on a riff on a riff of a **Piña Colada** (page 57), this cocktail takes that drink from the beach to the fireplace. It's also one of my favorite cocktail names I've ever conjured up. I long for the day that a patron asks me for "a Bit of Respite, please," and I'm able to provide that for them in liquid form.

While mint and orange juice are famous adversaries, with the mere thought of drinking OJ right after brushing one's teeth making many squirm with discomfort, the chocolate and coconut here bring them together in magical harmony.

The Bit of Respite is a classy cocktail for whenever you accidentally book your summer holiday in the Southern Hemisphere. It happens to the best of us.

INGREDIENTS

1¼ ounces (37.5 ml)
    funky rum (see *Note*)

½ ounce (15 ml) crème
    de menthe

½ ounce (15 ml)
    crème de cacao

2 dashes cocoa bitters

¾ ounce (22.5 ml)
    cream of coconut

¾ ounce (22.5 ml)
    pineapple juice

¾ ounce (22.5 ml)
    orange juice

Freshly grated nutmeg,
    to garnish (see page 28)

METHOD

Add the rum, crème de menthe, crème de cacao, cocoa bitters, cream of coconut, pineapple juice, and orange juice to a shaker.

Add ice and shake until chilled.

Dump (see page 31) into a chilled wineglass or hurricane glass.

Garnish with freshly grated nutmeg.

NOTE

Shoot for one of the funkiest aged Caribbean rums you can find here (Hamilton Jamaican Pot Still Black and Angostura 1919 are personal standouts).

Left: Amarolada; right: Bit of Respite ▶

Lake Ainsworth

● SMOKY   ■ BITTER   ▲ CHOCOLATEY

Dyed perpetually brown by the tea trees that line it, Lake Ainsworth in Lennox Head, near where I grew up, looks like a huge puddle of spilled iced tea or flat cola. Dubbed Coca-Cola Lake (not a sponsor), at least in my family circles, it was the place to be when I was a kid. Kayaking, swimming, and standup paddleboarding were the main activities, aside from the rope swing that was eventually taken down for safety reasons, much to our (the children of the Northern Rivers region) chagrin.

I've named this cocktail—a riff on a rich, smoky sipper invented by CJ Catalano called the Camp Maclean—after that wondrous place. It uses a mezcal rinse instead of the smoky Lapsang Souchong tea (if you're curious, see **Wishful Drinking**, page 182) and subs out the demerara syrup for the warmer cinnamon syrup to conjure memories of the colder afternoons in Lennox, though few and far between.

INGREDIENTS

Mezcal, to rinse
(see page 31)

2 ounces (60 ml)
rye whiskey

½ ounce (15 ml)
Averna amaro

4 to 5 dashes
cocoa bitters

¼ ounce (7.5 ml)
cinnamon syrup
(see page 24)

Orange swath, to garnish
(see page 27)

Toasted mini
marshmallows, to
garnish (optional)

METHOD

Rinse a rocks glass with mezcal and chill.

Add the rye, Averna amaro, cocoa bitters, and cinnamon syrup to a mixing glass.

Add ice and stir until chilled and diluted, 15 to 20 seconds.

Add ice to the prepared glass and strain the mixture in.

Garnish with an expressed orange swath and optional toasted mini marshmallows.

Postre Único

I hear you: This one sounds crazy. Coffee and savory tequila and smoky mezcal *and* chocolate *and* maple, all topped off with a layer of fruity cream. I get it, but hear me out.

. . . I've actually got nothing. This shouldn't work, but it so does. The raspberry cream dampens the powerful flavors that lie beneath just enough to make what could be an overwhelming drink one of the most pleasant, unique dessert cocktails I've ever tasted.

This one was inspired by El Chocolate, found in a "Coffee & Cocktails" booklet tequila company Patrón handed me at a mixology event. I found the original spec to be too bitter and lacking in sweetness for my taste, so I riffed on it. And so, Postre Único ("unique dessert" in Spanish) was born.

INGREDIENTS

3 ounces (90 ml) heavy cream

¾ ounce (22.5 ml) raspberry syrup (see page 24)

1½ ounces (45 ml) coffee liqueur

1¼ ounces (37.5 ml) tequila

¾ ounce (22.5 ml) mezcal

½ ounce (15 ml) crème de cacao

3 dashes cocoa bitters

⅓ ounce (10 ml) maple syrup

Freshly grated dark chocolate, to garnish (see page 28)

METHOD

To make the raspberry cream: Add the heavy cream and raspberry syrup to a separate receptacle.

Stir to combine.

To make the cocktail: Add the coffee liqueur, tequila, mezcal, crème de cacao, cocoa bitters, and maple syrup to a shaker.

Add ice and shake until chilled.

Double strain into a chilled rocks glass.

Float the drink with raspberry cream (see page 31).

Garnish with freshly grated dark chocolate.

NOTE

You can substitute a plant-based alternative for the heavy cream, but don't use "creamer," as I'm not sure I even know what it is.

Wishful Drinking

● SMOKY　　　■ FUNKY　　　▲ RICH

I'd been wanting to craft a drink using CBD for a while before purchasing a bottle of CBD bitters. The calming effects of the cannabinoid have always been fascinating to me, as I've never loved the feeling of being high but have *always* loved feeling relaxed. Combining alcohol with CBD creates what can be a gorgeous sensation when dosed correctly. If you're concerned about the effects of CBD, see the *Notes* section below for a more in-depth explanation.

CBD is paired here with sweet, funky Amontillado sherry and spicy rye whiskey that has been infused with intensely smoky Lapsang Souchong tea to form a drink where, somewhat surprisingly, every flavor is celebrated perfectly. Picture a **Manhattan** (page 48) that has been sitting by a campfire, on a quiet night, in the middle of nowhere, relaxed to the utmost degree, munching on some overripe grapes, and you've got the Wishful Drinking.

INGREDIENTS

2 ounces (60 ml) Lapsang Souchong–infused rye whiskey

1 ounce (30 ml) Amontillado sherry

5 dashes CBD bitters (10 mg CBD)

2 dashes aromatic bitters

Lemon swath, to garnish (see page 27)

METHOD

To make the Lapsang Souchong–infused rye: Add 1 Lapsang Souchong tea bag per every 4 ounces (120 ml) rye to a jar.

Cover and leave for at least 2 hours before removing tea bag and using the rye.

To make the cocktail: Add 2 ounces of the Lapsang Souchong–infused rye, sherry, CBD bitters, and aromatic bitters to a mixing glass.

Add ice and stir until chilled and diluted, 15 to 20 seconds.

Strain into a chilled coupe glass.

Garnish with an expressed lemon swath.

NOTES

- Sherry is a fortified wine. It often has a distinctively funky taste that I love. I'm almost always mixing with Lustau's Amontillado sherry.

- CBD, or cannabidiol, is one of the 113 identified cannabinoids in the cannabis plant (a.k.a. marijuana). Not to worry. CBD doesn't make you feel the "high" effects of weed. That is mainly attributed to THC, one of the other 113 cannabinoids. CBD and, in turn, CBD bitters help calm the mind and relax the body. I use Mountain Elixirs' CBD bitters. If you don't have access to CBD bitters or are uncomfortable using them, substitute 2 dashes of orange bitters.

Rosy Cheeks

SMOKY   ■ SPICY   ▲ TART

Excuse me while I get all cute. This drink holds a special place in my heart, as it is the result of a true collaboration between my longest-running (so far) boyfriend and me. Before meeting me, he was accustomed to drinking mainly beer and had never dabbled in the art of fine mixology or the tasting of fancy cocktails. Nevertheless, in the first months of our relationship he graciously allowed me to invite him everywhere I went. This was good because I don't love drinking alone and I wanted to spend every waking moment with him. Me being the avid drinker and cocktail "influencer" I am, the places he would accompany me were often either respected establishments or alcohol-related events.

He quickly caught on to this lifestyle and opened his palate to the world of cocktails, showing true interest in the field and seemingly loving the art of drinking and making drinks with me. Either that or he just liked me enough to lie about it to make me happy. We'll never know.

It became common in our household for him to make dinner while I made cocktails for us. One night, while *I* made dinner, I asked *him* to do *my* job, with a catch: He had to invent a drink on the fly. Hesitantly, he crafted a drink that was unique and surprisingly tasty! With a few tweaks, the Rosy Cheeks was born, named to emulate the color of the drink, the slight spiciness from the jalapeño, and the feeling he gave me when he walked in the door.

For other drinks crafted by/for this man, see the **10/10** (page 109) and **Floral Sex** (page 188).

INGREDIENTS

1½ ounces (45 ml) rose gin

½ ounce (15 ml) mezcal

½ ounce (15 ml) Benedictine

½ ounce (15 ml) jalapeño syrup (see page 25)

½ ounce (15 ml) grenadine (see page 23)

¾ ounce (22.5 ml) lemon juice, freshly squeezed

Candied jalapeños, to garnish (see page 27)

METHOD

Add the rose gin, mezcal, Benedictine, jalapeño syrup, grenadine, and lemon juice to a shaker.

Add ice and shake until chilled.

Double strain into an ice-filled rocks glass.

Garnish with candied jalapeños.

NOTE

This drink was crafted using Salcombe's Rosé Sainte Marie Gin. Feel free to find an alternative or just sub it out entirely for regular gin, perhaps with a few drops of rose water added.

8 Drops of Poison

● SMOKY   ■ HERBAL   ▲ FRUITY

This sipper is a riff on a Honolulu Cocktail No. 2. During a livestream, someone asked for "A Drop of Poison" and I ran with it, eventually renaming this drink to represent how many drops of "poison" ended up in the glass.

Where the Honolulu Cocktail No. 2 uses gin, this variation instead pairs smoky mezcal with the original's Benedictine and maraschino liqueur to create a richer drink. Peychaud's bitters subs in for the original's orange bitters to provide an aniseed-y note to cut through the sweet, smoky richness.

It's worth noting that you shouldn't use real poison here. Resist that temptation.

INGREDIENTS

1¼ ounces (37.5 ml) mezcal

1¼ ounces (37.5 ml) Benedictine

¾ ounce (22.5 ml) maraschino liqueur

1 dash Peychaud's bitters

1 dash Angostura bitters

8 drops maraschino cherry syrup

Lemon swath, to garnish (see page 27)

METHOD

Add the mezcal, Benedictine, maraschino liqueur, Peychaud's bitters, and Angostura bitters to a mixing glass.

Add ice and stir until chilled and diluted, 15 to 20 seconds.

Strain into a chilled coupe glass.

Add the maraschino cherry syrup.

Garnish with an expressed lemon swath.

NOTE

To simulate drops of "poison," I used the syrup from inside a jar of Luxardo maraschino cherries. Any red, syrupy liquid (grenadine, raspberry syrup, etc.) would work to create this effect, as it won't greatly impact the flavor of the drink.

Honey, I Made a Drink

● FLORAL   ■ BITTER   ▲ RICH

Every time I think of a cocktail name and don't yet have a drink to tie it to, it goes in my notebook. When I'm struggling for inspiration, I open that book to a random page, select a moniker, and try to run wild with it. The title of this drink was in that book for months before I finally got around to purchasing a bottle of mead (honey wine) and making what I wanted to call Honey, I Made a Drink since I wrote it down: a honey-based **Negroni** (page 53).

Dabbling in this endeavor proved slightly difficult, as which bottle in the simple three-ingredient recipe I would sub out for mead, if any, required some extensive testing. Campari clashed with the mead, forcing out a tasting note of old hard candy from grandpa's pocket, but Suze, a yellow, more herbal counterpart to Campari, worked wonders. Subbing mead for the gin made the drink too sweet, so the vermouth was chosen as the mead's tag team partner. The original equal-parts spec that a Negroni holds proved slightly unbalanced here, so a 3:2:1 ratio was used, making the mead the star of the show.

When a drink is finally perfect, after all that tweaking, the satisfaction one feels is immense. I love a Negroni. I love this drink. Put it in your mouth.

INGREDIENTS

1½ ounces (45 ml) mead

1 ounce (30 ml) Suze

½ ounce (15 ml) gin

Lemon swath, to garnish
(see page 27)

METHOD

Add the mead, Suze, and gin to a mixing glass.

Add ice and stir until chilled and diluted, 15 to 20 seconds.

Strain into an ice-filled rocks glass.

Garnish with an expressed lemon swath.

NOTES

♦ Mead is essentially a honey wine, made by fermenting honey, sometimes with added spices and botanicals. Dansk Mjød pretty much owns the market here. I like their Ribe Mjød, which uses apple juice in its blending, but feel free to experiment with whatever versions you can find.

♦ Suze is a bittersweet French aperitif, not dissimilar to the Italian Campari, but yellow and slightly more herbal, bitter, and earthy. It can bring a great complexity to drinks but, like most bottles made using the gentian root, can be fairly divisive. There's not many great substitutes for such a specific taste, but research dictates that Avèze is an acceptable swap here.

First Sight

● FLORAL   ▣ FRUITY   ▲ FUNKY

One of my favorite books of all time is *The Midnight Library* by Matt Haig. The basic premise is that, when one dies, they end up in this limbo space, somewhere between life and death. In this place, you can go back through your life's moments, regrets, and decisions and redo them to see how your life would have turned out had you made different choices. Haig's idea was that this limbo place would take the form of a location that was familiar and comforting to you. For the main character it was a childhood library, for another it was his uncle's video store. For me, I'm almost certain it would be a liquor store.

Don't laugh. I know. A drink-maker who likes liquor stores, shocker. But it's more than that. A well-thought-out, well-stocked alcohol emporium is ear-to-ear-smile-inducing for me. Whenever I'm having a not-so-great day or I'm passing by on a walk around town, a trip inside my local liquor store is enough to make that day that much better, even if I don't buy anything.

It was one of those escapades that resulted in me returning home with a tiny bottle of Snow Angel nigori sake one day in mid-May 2022. The bottle was pretty and I like cloudy nigori sake a lot, so grabbing it was an easy decision. That evening, I took a bottle of Japanese whisky, gifted to me by my friend Jaeden Martell, and a homemade strawberry-rose syrup I'd made for a previous drink (there's no need to make it yourself—just use strawberry syrup and a dash of rose water as mentioned in this spec). I chucked them into a mixing glass with the sake, all equal parts. What came out was a floral, funky, light, adult sipper of a cocktail that my then boyfriend and I guzzled before we could even name it. Then we named it. You get it.

INGREDIENTS

1 ounce (30 ml) Japanese whisky

1 ounce (30 ml) nigori sake

1 ounce (30 ml) strawberry syrup (see page 24)

1 dash rose water

Lemon swath, to garnish (see page 27)

METHOD

Add the Japanese whisky, nigori sake, strawberry syrup, and rose water to a mixing glass.

Add ice and stir until chilled and diluted, 15 to 20 seconds.

Strain into a chilled coupe glass.

Garnish with an expressed lemon swath.

NOTES

◆ Nigori sake is an unfiltered varietal of sake that appears cloudy (*nigori* literally translates to "cloudy") and has a floral yet deep funk on the palate. It's a fairly important component here, but feel free to try a different type of sake if it's difficult to find.

◆ Rose water is just that: water that has been infused with rose petals. It is extremely perfume-y and can be over-whelming, but when used in small amounts it brings a gorgeous floral note to a drink.

Floral Sex

On an evening in 2022, as I was cooking dinner, my then boyfriend decided that, for once, he wanted to grasp the mixology reigns. I happily obliged and handed over full access to my bar and refrigerator. He grabbed a bottle of clean junmai sake, rose gin, and hibiscus syrup and shook up one of the most floral, cleanest, most delicious cocktails I've ever tasted. I was truly blown away.

It took but a second to name the concoction, as our dirty minds prevailed in the blink of an eye.

INGREDIENTS

1 ounce (30 ml) junmai sake

¾ ounce (22.5 ml) rose gin

½ ounce (15 ml) hibiscus syrup (see Notes)

⅓ ounce (10 ml) lemon juice, freshly squeezed

1½ ounces (45 ml) soda water

Lemon swath, to garnish (see page 27)

Hibiscus flower, to garnish (optional)

METHOD

Add the sake, rose gin, hibiscus syrup, and lemon juice to a shaker.

Add ice and shake until chilled.

Strain into a small highball or Collins glass.

Top with soda water.

Garnish with an expressed lemon swath and an optional hibiscus flower.

NOTES

- While also referred to as Japanese rice wine, sake's brewing process is actually more akin to that of beer. That being said, its varietals are as vast as wine and each serves a different purpose. Junmai is best here for its clean and ever-so-slightly funky properties.

- Salcombe's Rosé Sainte Marie Gin was the original rose gin used when creating this spec. There are a bunch of others on the market. Most will only change the flavor profile slightly. You may also just use regular gin.

- I buy my hibiscus syrup, as procuring food-grade hibiscus flowers can prove challenging. The original spec used Sirop's, but most hibiscus syrups should taste similar.

Aristaeus

My first proper relationship after moving out to Los Angeles was a yearlong, long-distance one with a Greek guy who lived in Utah. His family was, as goes for every Greek family I've met, obsessed with good food and drink. Hosting dinners and caring for your loved ones seems to be an integral part of their culture, and I had *zero* complaints.

There are two Greek spirits that have been able to permeate America and other international realms, one being much more popular than the other. Ouzo is a divisive, aniseed-y aperitif, similar in flavor to the Italian sambuca. While I land in the camp of loving ouzo, I became more intrigued by the lesser-known (to me, at least) Metaxa.

The aged, brandy-based spirit is a deliciously complex addition to a bar and can be used in most scenarios where one would use brandy. It has an added sweetness that comes from adding aged Muscat wines, and a botanical quality brought by blending the distillate with a secret mix of plants and herbs. It blends with the honey and citrus in this drink to make something reminiscent of a Bee's Knees, a classic honey-gin cocktail.

While this drink was originally named after that boyfriend, it has since been changed to Aristaeus, after the Greek god of beekeeping and other food cultivation techniques.

INGREDIENTS

1¾ ounces (52.5 ml) Metaxa

¾ ounce (22.5 ml) elderflower liqueur

½ ounce (15 ml) lemon juice, freshly squeezed

½ ounce (15 ml) honey syrup (see page 24)

Lemon swath, to garnish (see page 27)

METHOD

Add the Metaxa, elderflower liqueur, lemon juice, and honey syrup to a shaker.

Add ice and shake until chilled.

Double strain into an ice-filled rocks glass.

Garnish with an expressed lemon swath.

NOTE

Metaxa is a Greek brandy-based specialty spirit. It comes in a few different bottles—3 Stars, 5 Stars, 7 Stars, and 12 Stars—indicating the number of years the sweetened brandy was aged in oak barrels. As with most aged spirits, the more years spent resting in barrels, the smoother the end product is. Take that into consideration when procuring your Metaxa. I try to steer clear of anything below a 7-Star. If Metaxa is unavailable, Southern Comfort is a slightly sweeter alternative, and any Cognac or Armagnac would be slightly drier ones.

Sloe Is Calm, Calm Is Sloe

● HOT   ▦ FRUITY   ▲ HERBAL

At the beginning of my drink-making journey, gin was my spirit genre of choice. My preferred simple bar order was a Gin and Tonic, a drink I eventually shared the true indulgence of with my mum, who now cites gin as *her* spirit genre of choice. Following her discovery, we started experimenting with infused gin, flavored gin, and its other close relatives, such as Pimm's and sloe gin.

While I've never tasted a sloe, a stone fruit not dissimilar to a plum, I'd like to think I'm fairly well-versed on its flavor after testing so many sloe-infused gins. Its deep purple color leads you to believe it will have a syrupy, berrylike taste, not unlike a crème de mûre, but the palate is actually much nearer the earth. Very, very rooty and reminiscent of the fresh soil used to grow berries, it blends superbly with the similarly earthy tea and the sweetness of both syrups here.

As my tastes have evolved and I've begun to prefer darker, aged spirits much more, very few drinks using lighter spirits—such as vodka and gin—have stuck around as go-to cocktails. The fruity, autumnal beauty that is Sloe Is Calm, Calm Is Sloe is one of those rare drinks. It has since become one of my preferred variations on the **Hot Toddy** (page 45). In fact, if you're lucky, you might just find me sipping one while reading a book in a bubbly bathtub surrounded by smooth jazz and enough candles to create a fire hazard. If you're lucky.

INGREDIENTS

1 ounce (30 ml) sloe gin

½ ounce (15 ml) blackberry syrup (see page 24)

¼ ounce (7.5 ml) cinnamon syrup (see page 24)

1 Earl Grey tea bag

4 ounces (120 ml) boiling water

Lemon wheel, to garnish (see page 27)

Cinnamon stick, to garnish (optional)

METHOD

Add the sloe gin, blackberry syrup, cinnamon syrup, and tea bag to a toddy glass or mug.

Add boiling water and stir with optional cinnamon stick to combine.

Garnish with a lemon wheel, leaving the tea bag and cinnamon stick in the drink.

NOTES

◆ This recipe calls for Earl Grey tea because of its calming qualities, but feel free to substitute with the drinker's favorite varietal. Chamomile, English Breakfast, peppermint maybe? You're *wild*.

◆ There are plenty of great sloe gins on the market—Elephant, Plymouth, and Hayman's, to name but a few.

Dreary Day's Night

I wasn't going to put this drink in this book.

Its mildly complicated recipe and unnecessary indulgence goes against most of why this book exists. Simplicity and minimal effort are its buzzwords, after all.

My opinion changed when it became my first drink to be published in a written work.

In late 2022, a magazine I'd modeled for in the past reached out to ask for a cocktail to spotlight in their upcoming holiday issue. Rattled and giddy, I sent them the recipe for a drink I'd just created a few weeks prior. Here is the blurb I gave them:

*There seems to be a group of classic cocktails I can't help riff upon (like the **Negroni** [page 53] and **Piña Colada** [page 57]) and every year, when Christmas rolls nearer, I try to switch up one of my faves, the **hot toddy** [page 45]. This specific variation blends a smoky Islay Scotch whisky with actual smoke from a flamed cinnamon stick, supported by the slight back-of-the-throat warming of peppermint tea, reminiscent of a candy cane. The addition of maple syrup in place of the traditional honey makes this drink feel even more indulgent while maintaining its prim and proper sleepy-time roots. Also, rosemary *weeps*. This cocktail is a campfire on Christmas Eve in liquid form, and isn't that just the loveliest?*

INGREDIENTS

2 cinnamon sticks

¾ ounce (22.5 ml) blended Scotch whisky

¾ ounce (22.5 ml) Islay Scotch whisky

¾ ounce (22.5 ml) maple syrup

½ ounce (15 ml) lemon juice, freshly squeezed

¼ ounce (7.5 ml) rosemary syrup (see page 25)

1 peppermint tea bag

4 ounces (120 ml) boiling water

METHOD

Break one cinnamon stick into pieces. Gather the pieces into a small pile and set it alight. Place an upturned toddy glass or mug over the top to smoke the glass. Let the glass smoke for 2 to 3 minutes. Scorch the second cinnamon stick and set it aside.

Add the blended Scotch, Islay Scotch, maple syrup, lemon juice, rosemary syrup, and tea bag to the glass, being careful to keep as much smoke in the glass as possible.

Add boiling water and stir with the second scorched cinnamon stick.

Garnish with the second cinnamon stick and serve with the tea bag still in the glass.

NOTES

- Smoking the cinnamon gives the drink a great aroma, but it isn't absolutely necessary here.

- Peppermint tea and whisky work phenomenally together, but any type of tea could be used here, all resulting in a different-tasting cocktail.

WHAT NOW? ▲

GOOD question. I'd imagine you'll probably stop reading this book? That's assuming you've read it from front to back, like a novel. An odd way to read a recipe book, but you do you.

If you've instead managed to read this like I imagine most people would, either concocting recipes you've found interesting as you've flicked through the pages or merely bookmarking them for later, promising to one day make them only to never make them ever, congrats, you're a normal person.

This book has been a labor of love and of thirst. I've pretentiously waxed lyrical about the drinks in these pages for many years now, and I'm tired. Grateful for and very happy with the result of my pomposity, but tired. My digits need a break from my computer's keyboard for a bit.

Before I go, I'll thank you, I guess.

If you're a beginner mixologist who used this book to learn the basics of drink-making through the whimsical eyes of a young boy such as myself, I hope you did learn. I hope you can now graduate to slightly more high-tech cocktail work and wow generations with your mixing abilities. I hope this book made you happy. Also, thank you.

If you grabbed this book from the shelf of an abandoned library as it sat gathering dust for years, what's the future like? Am I alive?

Find a way to contact me—I'd be interested in hearing from a futuristic, cocktail-minded bookworm such as yourself. Also, thank you.

If you're merely a fan of my work in one of the fields I've chosen to perform in and thought this book might allow you to get to know this pretentious Australian man a little bit better, I hope it did. I hope the life I've led thus far is even slightly as interesting as the life you're leading right now. I hope you continue in your interesting life. I hope you enjoy it. Also, thank you.

If you're under 21, or 18 in some countries, and you just read this book for the pretty pictures, give the book to your parents now. They need a drink after dealing with you all day. Also, thank you.

Thank you, truly. Being given the opportunity to put together a book that people may actually want to lay eyes on has been an absolute honor. The notion that you bought, borrowed, or stole this book makes me all kinds of excited. All kinds.

I'm gonna go away now. Not fully, just away from this book. It's yours now. I hope, throughout the remaining life you have left to live, you find time to drink at least some of the drinks that lie in the pages before this one. They're all very worthy of your mouth and your throat.

Thanks again. Bye-bye now.

—NH

ACKNOWLEDGMENTS ●

THE author (that's me, Nicholas Hamilton; I'm the author, hello!) would like to thank:

Mum and Dad. I wouldn't be living my dream now if you both hadn't let me do that from the beginning. Thank you for pushing me to be a greater success and a better person, even from so far away.

My best friend and illustrator, Mike Falzone. Thank you for your stupidly talented hands, your unwavering friendship, and your consistently above average Rocket League defense. You're my best friend and I'm yours, you've said that before. Horse.

My siblings. JJ & Suz, Bec & Alex (& Riley), and Rachel & Tyler. Thank you for your unwavering support regardless of how often I text, which isn't enough.

My chosen family. The people I choose to spend every day with. You guys know that I love you, I say it enough. If you don't know that, now you do. Thank you for keeping me sane and happy in this intimidating, beautiful city. Your constant presence is so comforting, and the love you show for me each and every day is palpable. Overwhelming, even. Tone it down. *Mwah*.

The creators and mixologists I have watched, listened to, and learned from for years: Anders Erickson, Cara Devine, Chris Leavitt (*Not Just a Bartender*), Dale DeGroff, Greg Titian (*How to Drink*), Hannah Chamberlain (*SpiritedLA*), John Rondi Jr. and Sr. (*Johnny Drinks*), Jon Kung, Jordan Hughes (*High-Proof Preacher*), Julianna McIntosh (*Join Jules*), Justin Sajda (*Thirsty Whale*), Kaitlyn Stewart (*Likeable Cocktails*), Lance Wong (*More Savory Goods*), Lucas Assis, Lui Fern, Miguel Buencamino (*Holy City Handcraft*), Sam Ross, Steven Roennfeldt (*Steve the Bartender*), and Wootak Kim (*BarChemistry*), to name but a few. Drink-making has opened my life to so many incredible opportunities and helped me meet some of my greatest friends. You were gracious, giving, and brought me in with a gentle hug and a shot of fernet, and for the first few things I'm grateful.

Everyone who made this book into a book! That includes, but isn't limited to, my astonishingly talented and efficient photographer, Brittany Conerly; the people at Countryman Press; Taylor Bourque; and other book-world people I'm surely missing out. All of you are the reason why the person reading this book is actually reading this book right now, and that's so nice.

To the people who inspired some of cocktails in this book. A handful of you belong in the above categories as well, but I'm gonna thank you again. Your existence not only made this book better but my life more colorful: Nan, Uncle Rossy, Gabe Escobar, H Woo Lee, Sofie Katsikiotis, and my TikTok audience. Thank you.

And to the man who inspired many of this book's recipes, who I spent some of the best years of my life with, Jackson. Thank you for sticking around. I will be forever grateful for the time we spent together. I can't wait to watch you grow.

And you! Thank you! Now, go! Drink! Bye-bye!

—*NH*

INDEX ▪

INGREDIENTS

cocoa bitters: Angostura Cocoa Bitters, 66n; Banane Noire and, 134; Bit of Respite and, 176; Bitters Sweet Symphony and, 139; Café Rouge and, 129; illustration key for, 36; Jaffa Kick and, 66; Lake Ainsworth and, 179; Postre Único and, 180; Santa's Nightcap and, 121; Tapsalteerie and, 69

coconut. See Coco Lopez, Coco Reàl, and cream of coconut

coffee, 20; Affogato Martini and, 125; Banane Noire and, 134; Espresso Martini and, 44; illustration key for, 37; Irish Coffee and, 46; Mezcal Dalnegroni and, 143; Post-Nut Clarity and, 137; Sundollar's Shaken Espresso and, 126

coffee beans, 28, 44, 125, 133, 134, 143

coffee liqueur, 20; Affogato Martini and, 125; Banane Noire and, 134; Café Rouge and, 129; Crème de Moka, 20; Crepusculo and, 135; Espresso Martini and, 44; Funky Russian and, 130; illustration key for, 35; Kahlúa, 20; Mr Black and, 20, 122, 130; Nectar of the Sods and, 133; No Takesies-Backsies and, 160; Post-Nut Clarity and, 137; Postre Único and, 180; Ressurection and, 138; Santa's Nightcap and, 121; Sundollar's Shaken Espresso and, 126; Tapsalteerie and, 69; Tempus Fugit, 20; Tia Maria, 20; Trips Abroad and, 140; Words Fail and, 122

Cognac, 19, 190n. See also apple Armagnac, apple brandy and brandy

Cointreau, 21, 169n. See also orange liqueur

cola, 37, 70

cranberry juice, 36, 41, 100

cream: Funky Russian and, 130; Flipsy-Doozy and, 170; illustration key for, 37; Irish Coffee and, 46; London Fog and, 106; Nectar of the Sods and, 133; Peanut Butter Grasshopper and, 174; Postre Único and, 180

cream of coconut, 20, 37, 57, 99, 169, 175, 176

crème de banane, 20, 35, 85, 94, 134

crème de cacao: Bit of Respite and, 176; Bitters Sweet Symphony and, 139; illustration key for, 35; Peanut Butter Grasshopper and, 174; Postre Único and, 180; Resurrection and, 138; Santa's Nightcap and, 121; Words Fail and, 122

crème de menthe, 35, 121, 176

Crème de Moka, 20

crème de mûre, 35, 40, 80, 94

Crème de Pamplemousse, 103n

crème de violette, 20

crème liqueurs, 20

cucumber, 28, 37, 73, 113

curaçao, blue, 35, 169

curaçao, dry, 21, 70, 169

Cynar, 19

Dansk Mjød, 186n

demerara syrup: Café Rouge and, 129; Crepusculo and, 135; Daiquiri and, 43; Funky Russian and, 130; homemade, 23; illustration key for, 36; Margarita and, 48; Mule Ride and, 154; Sazerac and, 58; Trips Abroad and, 140; Whiskey Sour and, 60

Disaronno:, 133n, 139n, 165n

Dolin Génépy le Chamois Liqueur, 105n, 109n

Dolin vermouth, 22

Don Julio tequila, 22

Drambuie, 19

Earl Grey tea, 37, 106, 117, 173n, 193

Earth, Wind & Fire, 170

egg, 20, 170n; Alstonville Sour and, 89; Apple Pie Sour and, 96; Banane Noire and, 134; Classy Boy and, 80; Eggnog and, 43; Flipsy-Doozy and, 170; H Woo Sour and, 108; illustration key for, 35, 37; Lonely Valentine and, 65; Me, Earl, and the Dancing Girl and, 117; Million Follower Cocktail and, 86; smell of, 27; Whiskey Sour and, 60; yolk, 20, 37, 170

elderflower liqueur, 20, 35, 73, 76, 79, 80, 190

El Silencio Espadín mezcal, 21

English Breakfast tea, 37, 45, 118, 173, 193n

Espolòn tequila, 22, 70

espresso, 126. See also coffee

Faccia Brutto Centerbe, 105n, 109n

Fee Brothers' Aztec Chocolate Bitters, 66n

Fee Brothers' Fee Foam, 20

Four Roses bourbon, 22

garnishes, 27–28, 35

Gelnaw-Rubin, Zachary, 145

Gibraltar glass, 33, 58, 149

gin, 20; Bramble and, 40; butterfly pea flower, 111; Classy Boy and, 80; Cuke of Lemonshire and, 73; Earl Grey-infused, 106; Empress 1908, 111n; Floral Sex and, 188; Haich Tee and, 146; Hamilton Island Iced Tea and, 70; Honey, I Made a Drink and, 186; illustration key for, 35; London Fog and, 106; Martini and, 50; Mum's Hum and, 79; Negroni and, 53; Philip and, 111; pink, 35, 79; rose, 35, 183, 188; Rosy Cheeks and, 183; Salcombe's Rosé Sainte Marie Gin, 79n, 183n, 188n; Tanqueray London Dry Gin, 20, 70; Whiskey Sour and, 60; You, Baby and, 83. *See also* sloe gin

ginger, candied, 27, 56, 150
ginger ale, 37, 74
ginger beer, 37, 52, 154, 165
ginger syrup, 25, 36, 56, 150, 163
Grand Marnier, 21. *See also* orange liqueur
grapefruit juice, 36, 85
grapefruit liqueur, 35, 103
grenadine, 23; Dirty Shirley and, 74; 8 Drops of Poison and, 185; French Bogan and, 159; illustration key for, 36; Lonely Valentine and, 65; Million Follower Cocktail and, 86; Read to Filth and, 164; Rosy Cheeks and, 183; Scofflaw and, 59

hibiscus, 36, 188
honey syrup, 24; Aristaeus and, 190; Dad's Tea and, 173; Greetings from Wilshire Green and, 114; Hot Toddy and, 45; illustration key for, 36; Lemony Trick-It and, 102; London Fog and, 106; maple syrup and, 21; Me, Earl, and the Dancing Girl and, 117; Penicillin and, 56
hot sauce, 37, 66

ice cream, 37, 125, 174
Irish cream liqueur, 35, 173

jalapeños, 25, 27, 36, 99, 183
jam, 37, 100
Jarritos, 70
Justin's Dark Chocolate Peanut Butter Cup, 166n

kombucha, 76n

Lapsang Souchong tea, 37, 179, 182
lavender bitters, 36, 106
lemon-lime soda, 37, 73
lemons and limes, 21
lemon vodka, 35, 118
Luxardo liqueur. *See* maraschino liqueur

M&M's, 137
maple syrup, 21, 36, 145, 180, 194
maraschino cherry syrup, 36, 109, 185
maraschino liqueur, 21, 35, 43, 83, 105, 185
marshmallows, 179
mead, 35, 186
Metaxa, 35, 190
Mexican Coca-Cola, 70n
mezcal, 21; 8 Drops of Poison and, 185; illustration key for, 35; Lake Ainsworth and, 179; Margarita and, 48; Mezcal Dalnegroni and, 12, 143; Postre Único and, 180; Rosy Cheeks and, 183; Woah There Mambo and, 99
milk, 37, 126, 166, 173
mint, 28; Cuke of Lemonshire and, 73; Grasshopper and, 174; Greetings from Wilshire Green and, 114; illustration key for, 37; Mojito and, 51; muddling of, 30–31. *See also* crème de menthe *and* peppermint tea

Nutmeg, 43, 46, 108, 117, 170, 176

orange bitters, Action Royale and, 76; Arnold's Plastered and, 118; Different Year and, 169; Greetings from Wilshire Green and, 114; Hamilton Special and, 156; illustration key for, 36; Manhattan and, 48; Martini and, 50; Moscow Mule and, 52; Old Fashioned and, 54; Philip and, 111; Scofflaw and, 59; Wishful Drinking and, 182n
orange juice, 21, 36, 44, 85, 90, 140, 144, 176
orange liqueur, 21; Action Royale and, 76; Bitters Sweet Symphony and, 139; Blue curaçao and, 169; B2P2 and, 103; Cosmopolitan and, 41; Debbie Did It and, 145; Different Year and, 169n; Drive My Sidecar and, 163; Gabe's Blueberry Cosmopolitan and, 100; Hamilton Island Iced Tea and, 70; illustration key for, 35; Jaffa Kick and, 66; Lazy Lucifer

sherry, 22; Alstonville Sour and, 89; Amontillado, 89, 156, 160, 182; Hamilton Special and, 156; illustration key for, 35; Lustau and, 182; No Takesies-Backsies and, 160; Oloroso, 89, 156, 160; Wishful Drinking and, 182

simple syrup, 23; Arnold's Plastered and, 118; Bramble and, 40; Eggnog and, 43; Espresso Martini and, 44; Hamilton Island Iced Tea and, 70; illustration key for, 36; Irish Coffee and, 46; Me, Earl, and the Dancing Girl and, 117; Post-Nut Clarity and, 137; Singing' in the Rain and, 113; Sweet Rum Rickey and, 155

Sirop, 188n

sloe gin, 35, 93, 95, 193

sloes, 93n

soda water, 22; Arnold's Plastered and, 118; Cuke of Lemonshire and, 73; Dirty Shirley and, 74; Floral Sex and, 188; illustration key for, 37; Lazy Lucifer and, 95; Mojito and, 51; Mum's Hum and, 79; Sweet Rum Rickey and, 155

Southern Comfort, 35, 74, 159, 190

sparkling wine, 33, 35, 103

Sprite, 73

St.-Germain, 20

strawberry syrup, 24, 36, 93, 95, 187

sugar cube, 37, 54

Suze, 35, 186

syrups, homemade, 23–25, 35. See also under specific type

Szechuan peppercorns, 108

Tabasco, 66n

Tapatío, 66n

tea, Australia and, 173. See also under specific type

tequila, 22; Crepusculo and, 135; Debbie Did It and, 145; Earl-Grey infused, 117; Hamilton Island Iced Tea and, 70; illustration key for, 35; Jaffa Kick and, 66; Lonely Valentine and, 65; Margarita and, 48; Me, Earl, and the Dancing Girl and, 117; mezcal and, 21; Nudey Rudy and, 144; Postre Único and, 180; Resurrection and, 138; Singing' in the Rain and, 113; Tequila Me Elmo and, 149; Woah There Mambo and, 99

THC, 182n

Tia Maria, 20

Topo Chico soda water, 22

Triple Sec, 21, 169n. See also orange liqueur

umeshu plum liqueur, 35, 111

vanilla extract, 37, 106

vermouth, 22. See also vermouth, blanc; vermouth, dry; and vermouth, sweet

vermouth, blanc: 35, 50, 94, 111n, 112

vermouth, dry, 35, 59, 109

vermouth, sweet: Attaché and, 112; Crepusculo and, 135; Flipsy-Doozy and, 170; illustration key for, 35; Manhattan and, 48; Mezcal Dalnegroni and, 143; Million Follower Cocktail and, 86; Negroni and, 53; No Takesies-Backsies and, 160n; Tapsalteerie and, 69; You, Baby and, 83

vodka, 22; Action Royale, 76; Affogato Martini and, 125; Arnold's Plastered and, 118; Cosmopolitan and, 41; English Breakfast-infused, 117; Espresso Martini and, 44; Gabe's Blueberry Cosmopolitan and, 100; Hamilton Island Iced Tea and, 70; illustration key for, 35; lemon vodka, 35, 118; Me, Earl, and the Dancing Girl and, 117; Moscow Mule and, 52

whiskey, 22; Apple Pie Sour and, 96; Axel Reese and, 166; Bin Chicken and, 153; cinnamon, 96, 122, 126; Clear Water Distilling and, 96n, 122n, 126n; Cupid's Chokehold and, 150; Fireball whisky, 96n, 122n, 126n; First Sight and, 187; illustration key for, 35; Irish, 22, 46; Irish Coffee and, 46; Jameson, 22; Japanese, 22, 187; Manhattan and, 48; Old Fashioned and, 54; Peanut Butter Grasshopper and, 174; peanut butter, 137, 166, 174; Post-Nut Clarity and, 137; ScandaLust Cinnamon, 96n, 122n, 126n; Skrewball peanut butter, 137, 166, 174; Sundollar's Shaken Espresso and, 126; Tullamore D.E.W., 22; Whiskey Sour and, 60; Words Fail and, 122. See also bourbon; rye; Scotch, blended; Scotch, Islay

yuzu juice, 36, 108

GENERAL